P

FILM STARS

Stars are an integral part of every major film industry in the world. In this pivotal new series, each book is devoted to an international movie star, looking at the development of their identity, their acting and performance methods, the cultural significance of their work, and their influence and legacy. Taking a wide range of different stars, including George Clooney, Brigitte Bardot and Dirk Bogarde among others, this series encompasses the sphere of silent and sound acting, Hollywood and non-Hollywood areas of cinema, and child and adult forms of stardom. With its broad range, but a focus throughout on the national and historical dimensions to film, the series offers students and researchers a new approach to studying film.

SERIES EDITORS

Martin Shingler and Susan Smith

Subhrajit Kar

Amitabh BACHCHAN

SUNNY SINGH

THE BRITISH FILM INSTITUTE
Bloomsbury Publishing Plc
50 Bedford Square, London, WC1B 3DP, UK
1385 Broadway, New York, NY 10018, USA

BLOOMSBURY is a trademark of Bloomsbury Publishing Plc

First published in Great Britain by Palgrave in 2018
This edition published by Bloomsbury India in 2018
on behalf of the
British Film Institute
21 Stephen Street, London W1T 1LN
www.bfi.org.uk

The BFI is the lead organisation for film in the UK and the distributor of Lottery funds for film. Our mission is to ensure that film is central to our cultural life, in particular by supporting and nurturing the next generation of filmmakers and audiences. We serve a public role which covers the cultural, creative and economic aspects of film in the UK.

(Previous page) Sanjay Bhattacharya's *Up Above the World* for B Seventy exhibition (2012)
Cover image © Dinodia Photos / Alamy Stock Photo

A catalogue record for this book is available from the British Library.

A catalog record for this book is available from the Library of Congress.

ISBN: PB: 978-93-88271-56-1

10 9 8 7 6 5 4 3 2 1

For Sale in the Indian Subcontinent only

Series: Film Stars

Printed and bound in India by EIH Ltd.

To find out more about our authors and books visit www.bloomsbury.com and sign up for our newsletters.

For Dad,

The real-life hero, although never the angry young man.

CONTENTS

ACKNOWLEDGMENTS

I was raised by a man who could ride horses, fly planes, shoot guns, and drive the fastest cars up the scariest mountains. A man who remained dapper in combat fatigues and grew dashing with a cocktail in his hands. For most of my childhood, I thought that he could do pretty much anything, just like the on-screen heroes played by Amitabh Bachchan. Over the years, I have come to recognise that, just like the on-screen heroes, he consistently stands up for the right things, no matter how hard and he has taught me to do the same. And like the on-screen hero, he sings and dances (the best bhangra dancer of them all), clowns about till we smile even in the midst of tragedy. And he loves, comforts, teaches, and nourishes. He is the real-life hero that Bachchan's screen persona can barely echo. So Dad, this book is for you.

I also want to thank my family: Mom, Rashmi and Siddharth without whom I would, and could, not write.
Love you guys!

Huge thanks to my agent, Laura Susijn, for being the best agent a writer could have, hope for, or imagine.

Finally, thank you Martin Shingler for all your support and advice throughout this project. I could not have completed this book without you.

1 INTRODUCTION

When an acquaintance's email showed up, frantically urging 'every Indian to vote' in a BBC online poll to determine the 'star of the millennium', the internet was relatively new to India, and online activism was unheard of. However, prompted by a combination of patriotism, cinephilia, and postcolonial urgency, I dutifully voted and was pleasantly surprised when the Indian superstar Amitabh Bachchan topped the poll, comfortably edging out Western screen idols such as Laurence Olivier, Alec Guinness, and Charlie Chaplin.[1] The BBC noted that 'Many people in the western world will not have heard of Amitabh Bachchan, 56, but he remains one of Bollywood's biggest stars, having appeared in more than 100 films in three decades.' (1999)

The BBC's explanation remains an inadequate summation of the star's trajectory over nearly half a century. Bachchan's career is also unique in terms of its longevity, impact, and reach, extending far beyond enduring cinematic success, and including a short-lived foray into electoral politics, a damaging but prescient entry into the corporate world in the 1990s, and a smooth, trailblazing switch to television and game shows.

However, despite the reams of film press and acres of celluloid devoted to Bachchan's professional and personal life, there are few comprehensive academic considerations of his star persona, the ways in which this serves as an expression of the zeitgeist, or the ways his filmic and parallel texts influence high and popular culture. Although scholars have considered Bachchan's star persona in specific phases (Mishra 2002; Prasad 1998; Sharma 1993) or examined specific social aspects (Poduval 2012; Rao 2000; Mazumdar 2010), there is no study of the full period of his stardom or of his effect on Indian cinema and culture.[2] There are no critical examinations of the ways in which Bachchan's star persona has been constructed and reconstructed through this entire time, serving at once as a site for locating contemporary Indian nationalism, a symbol of national aspirations, an object of sexual desire, an evolving model of postcolonial masculinity(-ies), as well as subverting and resisting multiple dominant narratives.

This book attempts to address this gap in scholarship by examining the complete span of Bachchan's stardom to date through the star's biography, screen persona, film texts, and secondary materials. His longevity as a star over nearly five decades of film-making, and the use of multiple media platforms, including film, pop videos, television, and digital media, make Bachchan's career and performances, as well as their reception, complex and unique. At the same time, his continuing career also renders this study – as any other without the benefit of chronological distance – necessarily incomplete. With Bachchan extending his career in different directions, including a television miniseries in 2014, there can be few conclusions about the ways his star persona will evolve, or the impact of his more recent work. This study attempts to examine Bachchan's stardom *to date*, and with full awareness that it shall inevitably be unfinished.

Before embarking on an examination of Bachchan's stardom, it would be useful to state my own location as a cinephile, fan, and scholar. As for many Indians of my generation, Bachchan has been a ubiquitous presence in my life. His first film, *Saat Hindustani* (Seven Indians, 1969), was released months after my birth. My first memories of my cinephile family include

A star bigger than the industry, *Kaalia* (1981)

vivid albeit confused flashes of scenes from *Anand* (Bliss, 1971) and *Reshma aur Shera* (1971). Both films also blend seamlessly in my mind with memories of the 1971 Indo-Pakistan war and the subsequent formation of Bangladesh.

For me, as for many who grew up with Bachchan's films, 1971 is only the first of many historic events linked in our memories with his films. India's first nuclear tests stood in stark contrast to his roles in *Majboor* (Under Duress, 1974) and *Roti Kapda Aur Makaan* (Bread, Clothes, Housing, 1974), with their themes of individual frustration and defeat in the face of structural oppression. The Emergency tallies with *Sholay* (Flames, 1975) and *Deewar* (Wall, 1975), and as tragic songs of resistance, perceived perhaps very differently through the lens of childhood than they were by adults. His films also suggested ways to confront socio-economic changes with *Trishul* (Trident, 1978), and narratives for dimly understood catastrophes such the Chasnala mine disaster with *Kaala Patthar* (Black Stone, 1979). His cathartic but increasingly narratively unstable, dystopic films of the 1980s, including *Inquilaab* (Freedom, 1984), *Main Azaad Hoon* (I Am Free, 1989), and *Agneepath* (Path of Fire, 1990) encapsulated tumultuous and seemingly catastrophic times. In retrospect, *Khuda Gawah* (God as Witness, 1993) seems not only a cry for 1970s-style secularism and co-existence but also a lament for an Afghanistan that had all but disappeared due to prolonged armed conflict.

By the end of the millennium though, Bachchan had reinvented himself as the successful entrepreneurial *pater familias*, and gave a generation of aspirational consumers his stamp of approval with *Mohabbatein* (Many Kinds of Love, 2000) and *Kaun Banega Crorepati* (Who Wants to Be a Millionaire, 2001, hereafter *KBC*). His innings in the new millennium defies logic with roles as varied as that of a married man in love with his daughter's friend in *Nishabd* (Without Words, 2007), a special needs teacher suffering from Alzheimer's in *Black* (2005), a Coppola-esque godfather in *Sarkar* (Ruler, 2005), and an ageing Shakespearean actor who must play one last great part in *The Last Lear* (2007). In addition, he has hosted multiple seasons of the television quiz show *KBC*, sold products ranging from shampoo to cars, controversially appeared in a television advertisement for Gujarat state tourism,[3] and developed a presence on social media, including Twitter.

For the generations who have grown up with Bachchan, his films – regardless of box-office success – provide a semblance of stability amidst dramatic change, help us explain and understand our world, and link real-life incidents, phenomena, aspirations, and desires to celluloid narratives. As a scholar, this life-long intimacy with Bachchan's film texts and stardom places me in an unusual situation. My study of Bachchan's stardom is simultaneously that of a scholar, a fan, and an individual whose key life experiences have been framed, shaped, and coloured by interactions with his star text and his overwhelming presence in the familial, social, and public spaces of my life.

At the same time, my position lies outside the two clear streams that dominate film scholarship on Hindi – and indeed, Indian cinema. Most Indian film scholars are located in urban, metropolitan centres with early access to technologies such as television, and non-Indian cultural products. A second set of scholars are part of the Indian diaspora with specific experiences of migration(s) and dislocations(s).[4] My childhood in small towns in northern India and remote border outposts means my experience as a spectator, fan, and scholar, places me on the margins of both these locations.

Unlike India's metropolitan centres, people in small towns continued watching films in cinema halls right through the 1980s and the 1990s, and televisions only arrived in the late 1980s, a corollary of Rajiv Gandhi's 'technocratic' policies. Economic constraints also meant that video cassette recorders were a late arrival, and even after they gained ubiquity, watching a film 'in the picture hall' remained an important social and familial ritual.

Confusingly, my father was posted to Islamabad, Pakistan during the early 1980s where Hindi cinema was passionately followed but officially banned. However video cassettes circulated abundantly and new films were available within hours of, or before, their release in India, allegedly through a complicated piracy network routed via the Gulf states.

In 1985, my family moved to New York, again as part of my father's job, and Hindi movies became a connection with India, a counterbalance to American television, films, and pop videos, and an assertion of a non-American identity. As members of the diplomatic community, we weren't 'diaspora' and were removed from some experiences of migration. Although the dislocation(s) of distance, language, and culture remained, they were diligently and assiduously addressed. However, one aspect of the dislocation was made more acute by both a scarcity of Bachchan films as his career began to wane, and the wave of new pretenders who hoped to inherit his crown. In some ways, Bachchan's wilderness years of the late 1980s and early 1990s reflect my own travels to far-flung parts of the globe, to corners where his name held little significance. Fortuitously, my return to India also coincided with the start of Bachchan's new innings in the public eye, first as the head of the film production and event management company, Amitabh Bachchan Corporation Limited (ABCL) and, after a few false starts, as the patriarch of Hindi cinema. As such, my own location – first as a small-town spectator and then as a marginal member of the Indian diaspora – informs my view of films and of Bachchan's stardom, but also positions me outside the two dominant streams of Indian film scholarship. At the same time, my location also replicates, in large measures, the demographics of Bachchan's primary – non-urban and north Indian, as well as international diaspora fandom.[5] In some ways, I believe, this particular location of simultaneous proximity and distance informs both the scholar and the cinephile in examining Bachchan's stardom.

Moreover, many of the key writings on cinema – and indeed, Bachchan – are by people closely connected to the industry. While this bestows the advantages of access, they also often lack a scholarly distance. This recognition guided my decision to focus on film texts and scholarship rather than on personal and biographical material. Moreover, an understanding of Bachchan's tightly controlled media persona means that I chose not to interview the star, as he has given ample interviews over his career and I doubted that another interview would deliver any new insights. At the same time, many studies of the star rely on a combination of reviews and interviews and often fall into fandom. Thus my focus on Bachchan's *oeuvre* is also guided by a need to clearly distinguish the fan from the scholar.

Prior to discussing Bachchan's stardom, it must be noted that while he is not Indian cinema's first star, he is its longest lasting one, occupying nearly half a century of India's hundred years of film-making. His longevity and predominance are also unique on a global level as his career has neither precedence nor parallel. Thus, any consideration of his stardom requires locating his personality, his films, as well as the secondary texts generated about him in a historical framework, especially as Bachchan's work is deeply imbricated with the national narratives and postcolonial imaginaries in and beyond Indian borders.

Bachchan enters cinema just over half a century after Dadasaheb Phalke's seminal *Raja Harishchandra* (1913). The intervening decades had established a tradition of film stars and fandom in the country. Moreover, Indian cinema had already benefited from technological advances, including early conversion to sound, as well as developing key themes, ideas, aesthetic and narrative conventions, and stars. Song books, records of music, playing cards, fanzines, and multiple other forms of secondary circulation had resulted in a sophisticated cinephile culture that responded and participated knowledgeably in the construction and maintenance of star texts, extending film viewing to a host of other cultural activities including dance, music, and fashion, and feeding into further films of particular stars.[6]

From early days, a range of male and female stars including Devika Rani, Nadia, Sulochana and PC Barua[7] provided the locus of on-screen glamour, desire, and aspirations.[8] A sophisticated audience consumed multiple film texts, often devised as star vehicles, and other media, cherishing film stars as 'national icons of beauty, desire and utopian beings' (Dwyer 2000: 118–19). Indeed, pre-independence India was dominated by female stars, its cinema organised around 'the female star as the primary attraction' (Prasad 2004: 106). Post-independence India saw a burgeoning of the film industry, and with it, a range of new stars, including the male 'triumvirate' of Raj Kapoor, Dilip Kumar, and Dev Anand who dominated the screens throughout the 1950s and much of the 1960s.[9] They represented three different types of heroes: 'Dilip Kumar arguably played the tragic hero who would rather lose his love than forsake his duty to his friend; Raj Kapoor was the romantic tramp who, like Chaplin, displayed strong melodramatic characteristics; Dev Anand was the consummate urban hero, a kind of postcolonial dandy, keeping up with whatever was the current aspiration of the Indian middle classes' (Mishra 2002: xiii). There were other stars too, especially in the tumultuous 1960s, including the boisterous Shammi Kapoor, the classically handsome Dharmendra, Sunil Dutt, and, Bachchan's immediate forerunner, Rajesh Khanna.

Between 1969 and 1972, Rajesh Khanna dominated the screen with his version of the tragic, romantic hero. A sensitive, romantic masculinity marked his roles, as did playback singer Kishore Kumar's melodious voice, which played a large part in Khanna's stardom. Khanna was dubbed the country's first superstar and inspired Beatles-like fan hysteria. He played the lead in Bachchan's early films, *Anand* and *Namak Haram* (Disloyal, 1973). But after Bachchan's *Zanjeer* (Chain, 1973), the national mood shifted dramatically against Khanna's gentle, tragic hero. 'After that the nature of the hero began to be defined in terms of the angry hero in rebellion...' (Mishra 2002: xiv). Moreover,

> Bachchan in many ways brought the tradition of the classic Bombay triumvirate (Dilip Kumar, Raj Kapoor, Dev Anand) to an end as he combined in his own cinema personality all the characteristics for which the 1950s triumvirate were famous: quiet melancholy, comic self-reflection, and urbanity' (ibid: xiv–xv).

If Prasad's 'birth of a new nation' marks a historical transition to the rise of the male star in India (2004: 107), the 1971 war was also pivotal in establishing 'the idea of the hero in total control of his destiny' (ibid: xiv), with Bachchan as its embodiment.

The 'history' of Hindi cinema is often located within a 'nationalist/postcolonial' discourse with a special emphasis on the films as a 'representation of the biography of the nation-state' (Chapman 2003: 323).[10] This – in turn – has led to the formation of a 'historiography' that links commercial[11] Indian cinema to the nationalist project and the nation-building exercise. Indeed, commercial Indian cinema inherits and circulates 'notions of national identity, negotiating conflicts experienced by the imagined community, producing new representations of the nation, and constructing a collective consciousness of nationhood through special cultural referents' (Virdi 2003: 7). Furthermore, cinema in India has often been coupled with the revival and regeneration of other art forms, and linked to an overarching nationalist project, although cinema 'of course deploys a unique apparatus that relies heavily on the other cultural forms imbricated in the nation-making process' (ibid.: 31). Bachchan's continued ubiquity in this filmic and extra-filmic history thus also becomes an overarching narrative, both on and off screen, for the nation.

Alongside this national 'historiography' it is necessary to take into account the formulations of postcoloniality(-ies) in filmic texts, and their reception both in and outside India. Indeed, commercial Indian cinema is 'a hugely successful global media form that has been strikingly successful in competing with, and sometimes dislodging, Hollywood in the global arena...' (Larkin 2003: 172). Most often analysed with regard to its popularity within the global South Asian diaspora, a closer look at Indian film's popularity amongst 'Arabic, Indonesian, Senegalese or Nigerian youth' reveals the 'extraordinary global reach of Bollywood – a cinema that has successfully marginalized Hollywood in certain world markets', in part because Indian films 'have succeeded in establishing a cultural and aesthetic style outside the dominant genres of American media', and often 'audiences engage with Indian films as a means of establishing distance from the ideologically loaded presence of American film' (ibid: 173). As Hindi films increasingly compete with Hollywood for global market shares, researchers are beginning to take note of the history of the presence of Indian cinema in markets as diverse as Russia, Kenya, Greece, or Turkey (Larkin 2003; Abadzi 2007; Behrend 1998, etc.).

In such diverse markets, the strands of postcolonial modernities, non-Western formulations of identities, and a search for alternatives to Western cinematic and discursive hegemony provide additional layers of complexity to Bachchan's stardom. Barriers of language, culture, even national polity, are overcome by fandom, and his star text is read and interpreted in myriad ways. If as 'complex signs embodying historical cultural and economic meanings, Bombay stars are cultural "compromises" of a bewildering complexity' (Mishra 2002; 126), any reading – especially of as long and diverse a career as that of Bachchan's – must also admit the possibility of a range of potentially conflicting interpretations. Thus it is imperative to recognise that his star narrative occupies the interstice of myth and national icon of desire, in addition to embodying multiple sites of contested socio-political identities in modern India and beyond. Add the struggles between urban/rural, Western/traditional, feudal/modern to the mix and his entire star text becomes a site of constant ideological contest. Yet it is precisely this centrality of Bachchan in the national cultural psyche for nearly five decades that makes any study both challenging and necessarily incomplete.

One reason that Bachchan's stardom is hard to analyse is the paucity of academic work on the specifics of stardom in Indian cinemas a whole. Although there has been an exponential growth in the study of Indian cinema(s) during the past two decades, to date critical analyses have primarily followed four tendencies: cultural/historical; technological; psychological/mythical; and political/economic[12] (Lutgendorf 2004: 3–4). Although these approaches are neither comprehensive nor necessarily incompatible, the first and the last have clashed mainly for ideological reasons (ibid: 2004). On the one hand there has been a tendency to overemphasise the 'traditional' angle (Dissanayake and Sahai 1992; Mishra 1985; Lutze 1985). On the other there has been an outright rejection or studious denial of any traditional aspect in favour of a politico-economic critique reliant on a questionable modernity (Prasad 1998; Dwyer 2002).

Two key examinations of Bachchan's early star text are divided along these lines, with one based on cultural archetypes (Mishra 2002: 138) and the second constructed on an 'aesthetic of mobilization' (Prasad 1998: 138–59). Mishra asserts that Bachchan's 'film persona challenged the figure of the noble, transcendent Rāma as the *dhārmik* model of the hero,' relying instead on the 'features that belonged to the antihero Karna in the *Mahābhārata* . . . .' (Mishra 2002: 128). On the other hand, Prasad emphasises the 'ordinariness' of Bachchan's roles explaining, 'Dockworker, mineworker, railway porter, police officer, small time crook: these were some of the roles Amitabh played in his career, roles that were predominantly lower class and integral to the evolution of the aesthetic of mobilization.' (Prasad 1998: 133–34)

Furthermore, some traditionalist scholars invoke 'classical tradition' and especially the two epics – *Rāmāyana* and *Mahābhārata* – as the 'founders of discursivity' in Indian arts (Mishra 2002: 4), and claim that 'any theoretical critique of Bombay cinema must begin with a systematic analysis of the grand Indian meta-text' (Mishra 1985: 134). These critiques have support within the industry, with Bachchan himself explaining: 'I believe leading men in Hindi cinema are indeed modern manifestations of mythical heroes from our two great epics…' (Kabir 2001: 26). However, while the two epics do provide a meta-textual reference for Indian cinema's themes or characters, and may be useful in considering the reception of film texts and stars, they offer little insight into the formal structures of cinematic representation. The 'cultural-historical' approach thus falters because an over-reliance on the epics emphasises the content and theme of films and ignores their structural, formal and stylistic elements.

At the other end of the spectrum, are the attempts to ground India's cinema in a localised, if questionable, construct of modernity that can be discussed from a primarily neo-Marxist position. This stream of criticism focuses on the political and economic organisation of the industry, debating both extra- and intra-textual narratives within their contemporary political contexts, while mostly bypassing the aesthetic and structural aspects of cinema.[13] Prasad's pioneering work argues that Indian filmmaking is rooted in the socio-political-economic conditions of the twentieth century and that films encode an ideology that 'subsumes' a modernising agenda of egalitarianism, individualism, and social change within a feudal and hierarchical model that perpetuates itself through the 'family melodrama' (Prasad 1998; Kazmi 1999, etc.). This line of study places the stars 'at the epicentre of Bollywood films, holding more importance than the directors, producers and all other aspects of the filmmaking process' (Varia 2012: 96). Stars became cinema's most valuable commodity due to the wishes of private financiers,[14] 'who believed that the safest way to minimise their risk on a film was to back films with a well-known star cast' (Gandhy and Thomas 1991: 112). By the 1970s, the dominance of the star was so entrenched that Bachchan – like other major stars – could have three or more films out at the same time.[15] Furthermore, the 'heterogeneous mode of production of cinema' ensures that, unlike Hollywood, stars can work on a 'shift' system, allowing them to make multiple films simultaneously. A closer study of the production process reveals the power certain key stars had in shaping their own persona and explains the proliferation of 'star vehicles' that showcase particular tropes associated with the star concerned, that have proven successful in the past. Although this line of enquiry provides crucial insights, by refusing to consider the historico-cultural aspects, it almost entirely ignores the intricate system of signs that is deployed to make meaning, and to construct and maintain star texts.

A third, 'technological' approach traces the distinctive features of Indian cinema to the new technologies of image reproduction during the second half of the nineteenth century, one strand of which confines itself to technical analysis of cinema itself, for example, analysing the camerawork and sound, dwelling on how Indian filmmakers have rejected Hollywood's 'invisible camera' style and 'centring' principles in favour of 'frontality'.

However, there have been few systemic attempts to apply these formal conventions to make meaning of cinematic texts,[16] even though some aspects, such as the examination of sound, mise-en-scène, costume, or camera angles may be deployed to great advantage for the study of stars and stardom. Bachchan's screen appearances, for example, reveal the clear encoding of specific cinematic techniques in multiple cinematic texts intended to enhance the brooding restraint and overt masculinity that define his star persona (Chakravarty 2013; Bhattacharya 2013). This line of research promises interesting insights into specificities of stardom in Indian cinema, although it has yet to produce a comprehensive study.

Given these *lacunae*, I attempt to follow Lal and Nandy's suggestion where 'the frameworks that combine the classical with the local and the contemporary would go farther and a new generation of researchers will produce more appropriate blends…' (Lal and Nandy 2006: xvi). As such, my study combines the methods outlined above. First, I consider Bachchan's star biography and screen persona, and their interactions over his full career. Second, I investigate the socio-historical elements that contribute to his screen persona and inform his star text, locating his cinematic texts as expressions of the zeitgeist. Third, I examine the mythico-cultural aspects of his screen persona and star text that shape the reception of his stardom and films among his primary audience and the ways in which extra-filmic cultural information is employed to make meaning within specific cinematic texts as well as over a range of films. Finally, I evaluate his impact on cultural production, including films, literature, and the visual arts. This method requires scrutiny of Bachchan and his films through multiple prisms even when discussing the same films and/or periods of his stardom.

Furthermore, I focus on the narrative, socio-political, and cultural aspects of his films and consider how these act collectively, and over time, to contribute to Bachchan's star persona and status. I attempt to analyse not only his career and stardom *to date*, but also to develop a possible model for the construction of star personas in Indian cinema by highlighting key film texts, and reading these in conjunction with and against the star's off-screen life and its narratives, the socio-political history of the country, and the culturally specific narrative paradigms, and semiotic systems. Although the constraints of this study limit detailed discussion of all the technical and technological aspects that contribute to formation of star personas, I refer to these when possible and necessary.

Therefore I explore Bachchan's key iconic roles not only in the films that were box-office successes at the time of their release but also in those that have grown in regard in secondary circulation due to his continued stardom. Reading film texts in their historical moments as well as through the lens of time suggests that enduring stardom can function as a 'success loop', conferring later popularity to films that may have initially been overlooked or forgotten. Moreover, the reception of such films may also offer insights that complicate star texts.

Chapter 2 outlines the star's biography in conjunction with his extensive filmography. It highlights the contradictions between Bachchan's 'star biography', based on accounts of his privileged upbringing as a member of the country's political and cultural elite, and his dominant initial parallel text that consistently positioned him as the underprivileged outsider. Covering films produced over nearly forty-five years, the chapter explores how these contradictions destabilised Bachchan's star text in the 1980s, as well as how they were abandoned in favour of narratives that attempted to address the new realities and, after a hiatus, were subsequently redeployed more effectively for the twenty-first century.

Chapter 3 builds upon the initial points of construction for Bachchan's star persona, placing key texts from the star's filmography at the intersection of historic moments of transformation in India's social, political, and economic fortunes.

By analysing the star in the context of national transformations, it explores how the star, his films, and stardom drew from, reflected and contributed to the national zeitgeist.

The fourth chapter traces mythical and religious imagery, building on earlier analyses of Bachchan's star persona as linked to the mythical figures of *Karna* and *Arjuna* and the extension of these to resonances of older, patriarchal figures in Indian/Hindu mythology, such as *Bhishma* and *Daśaratha.* It considers how Bachchan's repertoire of roles expanded with his reinventions, with narratives that reference his earlier persona but also subvert, extend, and expand it.

Chapter 5 examines Bachchan's star persona beyond the screen and Indian borders, and interrogates and outlines his impact on contemporary cinema and culture. It appraises his influence on formations of star narratives and cinematic performances of other, newer, stars and reflects on how Bachchan's iconic performances are continually referenced by filmmakers and actors through *hommage*, imitation and/or subversion. Finally, the chapter also assesses Bachchan's impact on cultural production in both high and popular spheres, including art and literature.

Attempting to examine Bachchan's full career to date is an intimidating proposition but crucial to understanding not only one of global cinema's most extraordinary careers, but also to begin theorising the specificities of stardom in Indian cinema. The current study hopes to explore culturally specific and context-sensitive ways of investigating stars and stardom, indicating potentially new and interesting aspects of research for film scholars, while also introducing the lay reader to one of global cinema's most important stars.

2 BIRTH – AND REBIRTH – OF A STAR

Bachchan's birth in Allahabad, on 11 October 1942, coincided with the Quit India movement, the last major mass agitation launched by M. K. Gandhi in a bid for independence. Although the movement was quickly crushed, it inspired his father, poet Harivanshrai Bachchan, to initially name his son Inquilaab (i.e., Uprising).[1] However, following fellow poet Sumitra Nandan Pant's suggestion, he decided on Amitabh, meaning 'enduring light'. (Bose 2006: 268).

Allahabad was, at the time, a key political centre for nationalist activities and the home town of the already powerful Nehru dynasty. It was also a culturally and socially progressive city with a 'vibrant professional and intellectual community which stoked the fire of social and political revolution' (Dasgupta 2006: 2). Acting legend Zohra Sehgal recalls that 'many inter-caste and inter-community marriages that would otherwise invite social resistance could be held there' (ibid: 2). Bachchan's parents were exemplars of the city's culture, combining nationalist politics, cultural production, and an 'inter-community' marriage.

Bachchan's childhood was typical of Allahabad, and other small north Indian towns of the time. Bose points that the

> family was not exactly rich: Bachchan senior earned Rs 500 a month and they neither had a fridge nor a ceiling fan, and in the intense northern

Indian summer heat, his mother would flood the floor with water to cool the room and place ice slabs before the rickety table fan to cope with the afternoon heat' (Bose 2006: 269).

This description however ignores the fact that 500 rupees was at the time a more than respectable salary and many upper-middle-class homes did not own fridges until well into the 1970s. If anything, the family was typical of India's politico-cultural elite and would, in the decades after independence, employ their position and connections to achieve economic prosperity and political power.[2]

Bachchan describes his upbringing as 'an ambience of East and West'.[3] His father was a respected poet, writer, and academic. His maternal grandfather had been called to the bar in London and his mother had been educated in a convent and had had an English nanny (Dasgupta 2006: 2). After independence, the family's closeness to the Nehru family served them well, with India's first prime minister sponsoring Bachchan senior's doctoral studies at Cambridge, and finding him a job as the head of the Hindi division of the External Affairs Ministry (Bose 2006: 269). The family's fortunes grew in tandem with the post-independence influence of the Nehru family and led them to Delhi.

The move to Delhi also opened access to world cinema. Bachchan has reminisced about watching films ranging from Laurel and Hardy to Satyen Bose's *Jagriti* (Awakening, 1954). Bachchan's cinephilia, and perhaps his ambition to star on the silver screen, seems to develop in these early years, and he mentions in particular Montgomery Clift in *A Place in the Sun* (1951), Marlon Brando in *The Wild One* (1953), and Charlie Chaplin's *Limelight* (1952). The family's friendship with the Nehrus allowed them 'privileged access' and they were 'invited to screenings of films at *Rashtrapati Bhavan*, the President's Palace', where he saw Czech, Polish, and Russian films. However, even then Bachchan felt the aim of cinema was not to preach, but to entertain (ibid: 269).

It is difficult not to consider Bachchan's early enchantment with Hollywood's greats as a factor in his own fame, or speculate about the ways these early films have influenced his own performances, and consider the ways in which his understanding and exposure to international cinema have interacted with his screen persona, as well as informed his consistent choice of films that privilege 'entertainment' over an overt social message.[4]

The family also had connections in the Hindi film industry, not in the least due to cinema's literary links. In addition, the Bachchans were 'very friendly with the Kapoors, film royalty' even in the 1950s and 'Harivanshrai would go to Prithviraj's stage performances and then, at the backstage soirées, recite his poems which Prithviraj liked' (ibid: 268).

After early schooling in Allahabad, Bachchan went to one of India's prestigious boarding schools, Sherwood College in Nainital. The school was also attended by Indira Gandhi's sons, Rajiv and Sanjay, and the three would remain friends until the deaths of the two Gandhi scions. Here, he seems to have preferred the sciences to the arts, with the exception of drama, winning the Kendall Cup (named after Geoffrey Kendall of the touring Shakespearean company), for his performance as the Mayor in Gogol's *Inspector General.*

Bachchan's academic performance remained lackadaisical at Delhi University's Kirorimal College, although he joined the college's theatre society, The Players, where he pursued his passion for acting. Soon after graduating in 1962, he moved to Calcutta (now Kolkata), taking up a job as a 'boxwallah', working in one of the 'managing agencies that the British had set up and which controlled a number of diverse companies' (ibid: 270). A combination of entitlement and discontent comes through in Bachchan's own description of these initial years: 'It was an ordinary run of the mill lifestyle, very mediocre' (ibid: 270).[5]

It appears at least part of Bachchan's discontent was due to his interest in the arts, especially acting. He continued participating in amateur dramatics, playing the part of Nick in *Who's Afraid of Virginia Woolf?*, and Cassio in *Othello*. He also applied and failed tests to work as an announcer, in Hindi and English, for All India Radio, a particular irony given that his voice would form an essential part of his film career and star persona.[6]

Yet there is little in Bachchan's biography that explains his decision to enter the film industry. The star has brushed off queries with the 'cryptic comment that he joined films because he could not get into the IITs and did not qualify for the civil services – a statement that can only be taken with a pinch of salt' (Dasgupta 2006: 1).[7] At the same time, he has noted that 'cinema in those days was something that was looked down upon. It was considered taboo in the so-called higher strata of society and by the more refined, educated elite' (cited in Kabir 2001: 110). Bachchan has also compared himself to his father, hinting perhaps at a sense of inadequacy: 'My father is immortalized in his work, while I am merely a cinema actor who will be forgotten with (the) passage of time' (cited in Raj 2010: 4).

The incomplete knowledge of his motivations 'limits our knowledge about how exactly he understood the world of the Hindi film, an understanding that probably shaped his image as a hero on screen in the days and decades to come' (Dasgupta 2006: 4). However, these initial nuggets of information about his life form key parts of his 'star biography', – for example, apocryphal stories tell of how he got his first film role with K.A. Abbas on the particular recommendation of Indira Gandhi[8] – and contribute to his evolving star persona over the decades.

A star is born

Accounts of Bachchan's arrival in Bombay (now Mumbai) are difficult to separate from his 'star biography' which highlights early struggles followed by meteoric success. There is evidence that Bachchan circulated photographs to various producers.[9] Although he reportedly did not attempt to exploit his family connections with film royalty, the Kapoors, he stayed with his father's friends in the city, although 'then, feeling he had overstayed his welcome, spent a night on a bench on Marine Drive' (Bose 2006: 271).[10] However, these connections ensured that his photographs did the rounds: 'Sunil Dutt had seen them, his wife Nargis had got to know Amitabh's mother and wanted to help, and B.R. Chopra had summoned him from Calcutta to have a screen test' (ibid: 271). However, Bachchan's unusual looks – he was considered darker and taller than the actors who had dominated the industry till then – seemed to rule him out for stardom.

Finally, he was hired by K.A. Abbas for his film on the liberation of Goa. While accounts vary – either he was recommended for the part or he wrote a convincing letter to Abbas – *Saat Hindustani* became his very first appearance on screen.[11] Bachchan is cast as a Muslim poet who joins a band of nationalists to free Goa from Portuguese rule. The film failed commercially although Bachchan's performance was critically acclaimed and won him the National Award for the 'best newcomer'.

Although Bachchan's role is relatively minor, with older, better-known actors taking up more screen time, he is hard to overlook in the film. In retrospect, the film contains vital characteristics of Bachchan's future on-screen persona, mixing a brooding, passionate intensity with poetic sensibilities, alternating between a quiet but explosive rage as the 'angry young man' and an emotional and dramatic quietude. Bachchan was reportedly intensely committed, even refusing a stunt double for a scene that involved him losing his footing over some rocks and dangling over a waterfall. The scene would have required a long shot with a body double, but as Abbas recalled, '…since it was him, I could zoom in and show the agony on the character's face' (Bose 2006: 271).

As poet Anwar Ali in debut film *Saat Hindustani* (1969)

After the film's critical success, Bachchan played a range of roles over the next four years, 'starring in as many as thirteen flops at the box office' (Dasgupta 2006: 7). He accepted negative roles, despite conventional wisdom that any aspiring 'hero' should avoid them, such as a murderous, obsessive lover in *Parwana* (The Lover, 1971).[12] His family contacts paid off when Sunil Dutt cast him in *Reshma aur Shera* as a mute sharp-shooter. His friendship with Jaya Bhaduri, then a big star despite her relatively short run in films, helped him secure roles in *Bansi Birju* (1972) and *Ek Nazar* (A Glance, 1972).

While Bachchan struggled to find his feet, the superstar Rajesh Khanna was posting one box-office success after another. Bachchan recalls that he had never seen such hysterical fandom: 'I think that the Rajesh Khanna phenomenon was different … in fact, in those days people used to keep trying to find words to describe Rajesh – "superstar", "phenomenon"' (Dasgupta

Unusual early role given Bachchan's powerful voice as the mute sharpshooter in *Reshma aur Shera* (1971)

2006: 8). This awareness of the Khanna 'phenomenon', led Bachchan to his first significant film, Hrishikesh Mukherjee's *Anand* (1971).

Bachchan knew he was in the shadow of this superstar ... and he deliberately decided to play the doctor who looks after the dying cancer patient, Anand, played by Khanna in the film ... Bachchan's motivation was that if he played off the super star he would get some attention' (Bose 2006: 273).

This high-risk strategy promised screen time but also possible relegation to second-fiddle roles, although Bachchan viewed it in positive terms: 'The very fact that I'd been teamed with Rajesh Khanna, the greatest idol, gave me a semblance of importance and respectability' (ibid: 273). Indeed, the film brought Bachchan

Early hint of the Anthony Gonsalves in *Bombay to Goa* (1972)

more critical acclaim, and he received his first Filmfare Award, for Best Supporting Actor. However, it also threatened to pigeonhole him into 'character' parts, and further distance him from potential stardom.

In retrospect, *Anand*'s taciturn, sensitive doctor appears to be another building block in the star's developing screen persona. He is positioned as the dark to Khanna's light, his hooded eyes and brooding demeanour in stark contrast to the laughing, joyful, dying man, and these same tightly leashed passions would develop – in successive films – into the persona of the slow-burn angry young man.

Moreover, Bachchan also saw glimmers of box-office success with Mehmood's *Bombay to Goa* (1972), a low-budget action-comedy caper where he danced, fooled around, and threw a few punches. With his infectious enthusiasm and boundless energy, the film's Ravi is the forerunner to the actor's iconic 1977 role of Anthony Gonsalves.

Again, Bachchan's casting was a combination of luck and networking: he had befriended Mehmood's brother, Anwar Ali, cast as the driver in the film. The friendship had led to Bachchan's becoming a paying lodger in the director's home. The combination of friendship and a small budget probably helped in his casting.

The film's commercial success was credited mainly to Mehmood's comedic skills as Bachchan's lead was incidental rather than central to the narrative. However, 'it was the way Amitabh carried himself in this film that influenced director Prakash Mehra and writers Salim-Javed to sign him up for *Zanjeer*' (Dasgupta 2006: 9). Mehra had already approached Dev Anand, Raj Kumar, Dharmendra and Rajesh Khanna for the role and all had turned it down for various reasons (Bose 2006: 275). At the suggestion of Pran, who had been cast as the Pathan, Mehra and his scriptwriters, Salim and Javed, went to see *Bombay to Goa*:

> The film had a fight scene and the moment Mehra saw it he screamed "*Mil Gaya*," meaning "We have got it." While the rest of the audience in that hall turned to look at him in surprise, Mehra got up and walked out – he did not need to see the film till the end – and, as he did so, he told Javed, "We have found our hero"' (ibid: 275).

Despite the grim run-up to the release of the film – Bachchan's thirteenth film, *Bandhe Haath* (Tied Hands, 1973) had also failed at the box office – *Zanjeer* would change the fortunes of not only its leading star but also Mehra and the film's scriptwriting duo Salim-Javed, none of whom had a track record of commercial film successes.[13] Indeed, there was little in the film's production values or team that suggested it would be an immediate success nor garner its iconic status: '*Zanjeer* was a cheap production with poor sets, no star value, and narrative ingredients that, until then, had been deemed to appeal

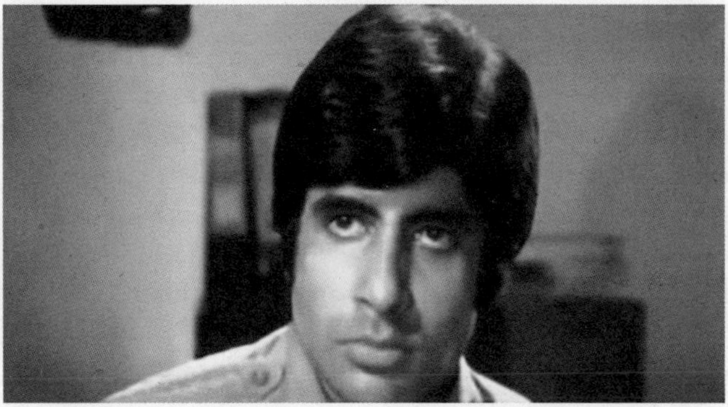

Zanjeer (1973) and the birth of the 'angry young man'

exclusively to a larger but unofficial market at the lower end of the industry' (Vitali 2008: 191). Bachchan was cast because 'as an ordinary actor devoid of melodramatic skills, he was a cheap, "good looking" male body available within the central to upper end of the market' (ibid: 191). However, Bachchan's critical acclaim from earlier films gave him a 'social' cachet not usually affordable for low-budget productions. The risky strategy of appearing with the reigning star, Khanna, had given him, if not star status, then at least the 'semblance of importance and respectability' that could attract middle-class audiences who had not – in significant numbers, at least – thus far patronised action films.

Zanjeer was also different from other low-budget films as its dearth of star power meant the film relied heavily on the script:

> *Zanjeer*'s script systematized the incorporation into the film of selling points that had proved their effectiveness in the large, lower end of the market, adapting them to some of the generic requirements of the industry's central stream, including the construction of a distinctive star persona and character persona suitable for future exploitation (ibid: 192).

The film established Salim-Javed as successful scriptwriters, heralding a 'new' form of scripting in Hindi cinema and beginning a partnership with Bachchan that would continue over a series of hugely successful films through the 1970s and 1980s. For Bachchan, *Zanjeer* initiated a stardom that endures to this day and established the foundational text of his star persona as the 'angry young man'.[14] After *Zanjeer*, all the characteristics that had previously been critiqued as disadvantages were admired:

> Amitabh's physiognomy, his slightly emaciated look suited the new image of the hero. His thin face made him appear meditative and lean body, active. His lanky figure conveyed a litheness of spirit, the sunken eyes now seemed deep and reflective, and his high cheekbones and a jawline that jutted out signified character and determination. In later films, this had an impact on the way sets would be lighted. We would not yet have backlighting but we would have a few more shades in place of the usual surgical lighting (Dasgupta 2006: 18).

Zanjeer began one of the longest success streaks in Indian cinema as Bachchan delivered back-to-back hits with *Namak Haram* – again playing the second lead to Khanna's superstar – *Sholay*, *Deewar*, *Kabhie Kabhie* (Sometimes, 1976), *Amar Akbar Anthony* (1977), *Don* (1978), *Trishul*, *Muqaddar ka Sikandar* (Emperor of Fate, 1978). So prolific and successful was Bachchan in this period that he was working on multiple films at the same time and, at any given time, had multiple films showing on screens across the country. His presence was seen as a guarantee for commercial success, and not without reason:

> Of the seventy-odd films he starred in from 1973–1984, when he took a sabbatical from films to enter politics, only three failed to recover their costs. A 1984 survey showed that of the fifteen all-time top gross films in Hindi cinema, 40% starred Bachchan. Even those films

considered flops at the time of their initial release, went on to become successful when re-released. In fact, some of his films made more money on re-releases than many a hit film starring other actors (Bose 2008: 276).

His success was so meteoric and encompassing that he made the cover of *India Today* on 1 May 1980 with the headline: 'The One-Man Industry'. In 1989, *Filmfare* magazine reflected on Bachchan's success:

The distance between him and his rivals was so vast that in the number game, they'd allotted the numbers 1 to 10 to him, the competition really took place way down there and it never affected the big man at the top' (1989: 38; cited in Chakravarty 1993: 230).

Zanjeer also marked a turning point in Bachchan's personal life. He married Jaya Bhaduri,[15] who had supported him in his early career, and had appeared in *Zanjeer* in the role of a street-wise knife-sharpener. Bose notes that Bachchan would present the actress with expensive saris, 'most of them were white, with a purple border, a colour Jaya hated but she wore them nevertheless so as not to upset him' (2006: 275). That minor detail provides a telling glimpse into the Bachchan marriage as well as the public narrative that coalesced around it in subsequent years. The couple acted together in films like *Abhimaan* (Pride, 1973), *Chupke Chupke* (Quietly/Discreetly, 1975), *Sholay*, and *Mili* (1975), and the controversial *Silsila* (The Affair, 1981).[16] With the notable exception of *Sholay*, all these films are closer to Bhaduri's preferred genre of 'parallel cinema' with a focus on realist narratives and a world away from the films that propelled Bachchan's screen success.

The couple had two children, a daughter in 1974, and a son in 1976, and Bhaduri continued to appear in films throughout the 1970s, although Bachchan's star biography suggests she quit

Angry young man. *Deewar*

cinema soon after marriage. However, most of Bachchan's films required a different kind of co-star, one who could add a glamorous edge to the actor's passionate intensity. A narrative grew around the marriage, of a controlling superstar who gently pushed his wife off screen, with even Bachchan declaring that in marrying Jaya he had 'deprived the Indian screen of a fantastic actress' (Mishra 2002: 132). Meanwhile, as Bachchan's films became ever-more high budget and glamorous, rumours swirled of romances with various female stars, including Zeenat Aman, Parveen Babi and, most persistently, Rekha. Bhaduri did not scotch these rumours, commenting cryptically that 'women have always been a problem with Amit. It was so, even when he was not a star' (ibid: 132). In Bachchan's star biography, and despite rumours of extramarital affairs, the narrative of stable marriage, a retiring wife, and the 'stability' of the family unit appear intended to counter his usually rebellious on-screen persona.

This clash of socially conservative values with on- and off-screen avowals of rebellion should destabilise both his star persona and 'star biography'. However, as I suggest in Chapter 3, this very dichotomy may hold the key to understanding Bachchan's longevity as a star, as he embodies the contradictions of modernity in the country, and beyond. This incongruity may explain Bachchan's claim that 'There seems to be a strong sense of revolt within me', while simultaneously asserting that 'Probably it is in my genes. I have seen rebellion in my father's writing, in his early life…' (cited in Mishra 2002: 128).

The meteoric rise and rise of a superstar

The following years of Bachchan's career are packed with a dizzying list of iconic films and are significant in the initial construction of his star persona, with two recognisable points of entry: the 'angry young man' of the action films, and the 'middle-class' protagonist of Hrishikesh Mukherjee's brand of cinema (see Prasad 1998). The latter belonged to the 'parallel' cinema of the 1970s, characterised by small budgets, a neo-realist aesthetic, distinct social concerns, and narratives that often focused on the country's growing middle class. The twin images helped Bachchan cement his stature as more than an 'action star', with cross-class appeal. Moreover, they also drew on each other to expand his range of roles: *Hera Pheri* (Monkey Business, 1976) augments the *Bombay to Goa* persona, while Mukherjee's *Chupke Chupke* casts him as a geeky English professor, exploiting a previously unmined comic streak. The two strands would frame Bachchan's growing star persona, until the 'epic'[17] films – from 1977 onwards – would unite them in a single all-encompassing image that combined the sensitivity of the middle-class protagonist and the comic timing and unbound enthusiasm from *Bombay to Goa* with the barely restrained fury of the 'angry young man'.

However, by 1977, the middle-class protagonist would also disappear as Bachchan's star power continued to increase. Presciently, Mukherjee had cast him opposite Khanna in *Namak*

Haram as the spoiled son of an industrialist. The easy arrogance that Bachchan brought to the role had hinted, far more than any other film until then, at his privileged upbringing. This was now bolstered by his own individual achievements. After *Namak Haram*, Bachchan's ability to sustain the awkward, reserved 'middle-class' persona seems to diminish, and even when he plays a nominally 'average' man – in films like *Manzil* (Goal, 1979) or a rural bumpkin in *Don*, the character's subaltern location is merely a narrative device and temporary disguise.

As his stardom grew, in public at least, the star presented an appropriately socially conservative persona, first giving up cigarettes, and then becoming a teetotaller and a vegetarian (Dasgupta 2006: 18). There is some evidence that Bachchan has been fully cognisant of and involved in actively shaping and controlling the extra-filmic narrative of his life and screen career.[18] The industry publicity machine provided 'fanzines with a continuous barrage of information: his relations to other stars (male and female), his relations to "starlets" (the ultimate commodity), his achievements in stunts ... used to confirm his masculinity...' about the star (Mishra 2002: 130). It seems plausible that 'Bachchan consciously cultivated a screen biography of the aggressive underdog, and a personal, real-life biography of a disquieting, dark, brooding spirit drawn toward beautiful women as some kind of aesthetic act' (ibid: 131). Bachchan's family was also deployed to support this idea, with his parents, wife, and children appearing in his occasional ruminations – almost always framed in terms that drew on aspects of his star persona.[19]

However, even a star like Bachchan could not remain immune to the turmoil the Emergency brought to the country and to him personally. As Indira Gandhi's government crushed press freedoms, journalists began to find ways of resisting the state: 'One way was to stop writing about Bachchan in retaliation, as it was felt that being close to the Gandhis, and in particular Sanjay Gandhi, he was behind the censorship' (Mishra 2002: 298).

Bachchan was predictably upset although his reaction is also revealing:

> During the Emergency, a feeling arose in the film media that its imposition was my doing … because of my family's friendship with Mrs. Indira Gandhi. Without cross-checking the facts, a ban was clamped on me. I wasn't to be written about and my photographs weren't to be printed in the film press. I felt this was wrong; that this was a form of misrepresentation. If the press had the liberty to ban me, I had the liberty to ban them (cited in Mishra 2002: 299).

Despite Bachchan's close association with the Gandhi family, it is notable that none of his films released during the Emergency[20] suffered. If anything, the apparent film press 'ban' contributed to his star power. Moreover, he continued to receive enormous attention in the national media, including political, news, and lifestyle press, just not from the film gossip and fan magazines. However, this also provided the star with a measure of privacy, with the advantage that he did not need to address any of the rumours that were printed about him.[21] During this period, Bachchan consolidated his public mystique, enhanced control over his personal privacy, while also astutely using the 'ban' to further the conflation of his personal life with his on-screen persona as the embattled underdog and loner.

It is also in this period that Bachchan's developing star text collides with another rising star: Rekha. The daughter of Gemini Ganesan, one of the biggest south Indian film stars, Rekha had made her debut in Hindi cinema in 1970 and subsequently achieved fame as a gawky, poorly made-up actress in B-grade films. The two stars met on the set of *Do Anjaane* (Two Strangers, 1976), an off-beat 'thriller' with Rekha playing a woman desperate to become a film star. The film had little significant impact on Bachchan's career or star persona, although it benefited from his pull at the box office. With poor production values and a small budget, the film is forgettable for everything except for

Bachchan and Rekha in *Silsila*, the last film the two made together

marking one of the most fascinating episodes of the constructions of star texts in cinema.

In the following years, the pair would act in a series of box-office hits including *Khoon Pasina* (Blood and Sweat, 1977), *Muqaddar ka Sikandar* (Emperor of Fate, 1978), and *Mr. Natwarlal* (1979), becoming one of the most successful screen couples in Indian film history. The potentially sordid aspect of the rumoured, extramarital affair was offset by the actress's *Pygmalion*-like on-screen transformation from an unrefined sex symbol to a sophisticated star (Dasgupta 2006: 51).

Mishra notes that the 'star is thus not simply a screen image; he or she is also a product of a fanzine culture that successfully conflates film and real lives' (2002: 141). In this case, both stars actively melded filmic and real lives, not only through fanzines and interviews but also in their film choices. In her interviews, Rekha often spoke about a famous 'Him' that she loved, making frequent oblique references to 'his silences' and how she could understand them.[22] At the same time, despite his silence, Bachchan was 'aware of the importance of the relationship and its use in the fanzines as a crucial component of his own image as a star' (ibid: 141).

Given Bachchan's 'ban' on film press, Rekha's statements could not be verified and instead '…added to his allure and to an even more extensive treatment of the relationship in the fanzines' (ibid 2002: 141). Moreover, the actress actively and flawlessly echoed some of Bachchan's famous mannerisms, referencing his body language and diction in films like *Khoobsurat* (Beautiful, 1980). 'Over time, people saw in Rekha the feminine avatar of Amitabh… She also had enough erotic appeal onscreen to be able to lure the characters Amitabh played, almost all of whom seemed to be immune to corporeal corruption' (Dasgupta 2006: 51). Indeed, Rekha effectively employed her ability to mirror Bachchan in a series of action-revenge films of the 1980s and 1990s, including *Khoon Bhari Maang* (Blood Marriage, 1988) and *Phool Bane Angaarey* (Flowers Became Embers, 1991).

Unsurprisingly, given their active use of aspects of their real life to further their star texts, at the height of the press frenzy, Bachchan and Rekha made one final, and daring, screen appearance: *Silsila* '…avowed through fiction what the stars disavowed in the real world: the triangular relationship of Jaya Bhaduri, Amitabh and Rekha'[23] (Mishra 2002: 141). Bachchan and Bhaduri played a stable, if unhappily married couple, while Rekha played the tempestuous and also married lover. The film was not a success at its release although it has since grown in both popularity and critical acclaim, in part due to the continued interest in the 'so called "real life" triangle' (Dwyer 2002: 128).

Scriptwriter Javed Akhtar blames the film's failure on a weak script: 'After picking a bold theme on extra-marital relationships, Yash Chopra develops cold feet, and the film becomes apologetic… probably because he wasn't convinced of the moral stand he himself had taken' (cited in Dwyer 2002: 127). Despite its box-office failure, *Silsila* became a vital point in the star biographies of both stars, perhaps more so because the two would not reunite on screen after the film.

Real life meets reel life. *Silsila* (1981)

Near death, and resurrection

The off- and on-screen drama of the love triangle, however, would soon be overtaken by a more momentous event. On 25 July 1982, Bachchan was injured in Bangalore[24] while shooting for Manmohan Desai's *Coolie* (Porter, 1983). The shot required a simulated punch to the star's abdomen, a fall on a desk, followed by a half-somersault to the other side of the desk. Bachchan refused a body double and shot the sequence himself. The first shot, with actor Puneet Issar, was deemed successful but Bachchan soon complained of pain. Shortly after, the actor was taken to hospital, first in Bangalore, then to Mumbai's Breach Candy hospital, as his condition mysteriously deteriorated. Doctors finally identified septicaemia as a result of a minor injury. On 2 August 1982, Bachchan was declared clinically dead at the hospital, rapidly revived and was miraculously on the road to recovery. These are the facts at least. Beyond that, real life, film, and stardom collapse into a seamless whole.

Near death. And revival. *Coolie* (1983)

Bachchan's accident marked a moment of mass hysteria in India and abroad, a demonstration of both star power and the influence of a star on public discourse and imagination. As the star lay in hospital, rumours grew, with some accusing Issar of deliberately attacking the star.

> Others changed the fifteen-second sequences into a complicated fight sequence in which fists as well as legs were used. The hero's fall was magnified into a twenty-foot fall. Amitabh Bachchan's screen presence as the indestructible hero made people think that only an extraordinary event could have led to his injury (Mishra 2002: 143).

The mass hysteria was partly fuelled by the media. The hospital instituted a daily bulletin which was carried by the national press. *The Times* correspondent in India, Trevor Fishlock wrote:

> Public prayer meetings were called and people gathered in their thousands to plead for him. Advertising hoardings were rented to carry messages urging the hero to survive . . . . Hospital bulletins on his condition were front-page news every day and newspapers and magazines carried large articles (cited in Bose 2006: 323).

In a real-life imitation of many Bachchan-Desai films, prayers were offered in temples, mosques, churches, and *gurudwaras*, and crowds thronged outside the hospital for news of their idol. Visitors included the biggest stars of Indian cinema including Zeenat Aman, Shashi Kapoor, and Amjad Khan. Bachchan's elite connections were very much in evidence as 'Rajiv Gandhi cut short his American trip to see his friend in hospital on August 5. Prime Minister Indira Gandhi, too, made a "purely personal and private" visit' on 8 August (ibid: 144). All the while, journalists and fans waited for Rekha, the star's rumoured lover. But she never came.

Upon his recovery, Bachchan himself added to the filmic narrative:

> On August 2 (1982) I was declared clinically dead. Jaya had gone to the Sidhi Vinayak temple and she rushed back. Panic-stricken she stood outside the ICU (intensive care unit), watching the doctors' attempts to revive me ... apparently in vain. Suddenly she screamed from outside. Don't give up, I just saw his toe move. Please keep trying. The doctors started massaging my feet upwards. And I came back to life (cited in Mishra 2002: 142).

The above passage assembles many of the elements of Bachchan's blockbuster films: a devoted wife; a trip to the temple; a near miracle when doctors had apparently given up;[25] and in a elision of star and divinity, the 'massaging of feet' recalls episodes from the Hindu epics of the care bestowed by humans on deities, with the doctors now reframed as devotees.[26]

Bachchan recovered fully and reported back to the set of *Coolie* on 7 January 1983. The shooting resumed with the sequence that had been interrupted by his accident. National media and billboards across the country celebrated the star's return to work, proclaiming 'God is Great! Amitabh Lives'.[27]

The amalgamation of the star's on-screen and real-life experience did not end with his return to acting as the film's script was amended to include the actor's near-death experience. Although Desai, as director, 'deplored the morbid publicity – "publicity not paid for by me", as he said' he chose to 'satisfy' the public (Haham 2006: 51).

In the film, two freeze frames are included to inform the viewer of the punch that caused the injury. Printed on the screen in three languages, English, Hindi, and Urdu, are words that explain: 'This is the shot in which Amitabh Bachchan was seriously injured.' Indeed, with this device, 'the hero of our time becomes pure simulacrum' (Mishra 2002: 144). Haham is more empathetic, noting that

> the intervention of reality in the midst of a screen story might seem an unnecessary distraction, but for the masses of India who had prayed for Amitabh Bachchan's recovery, Manmohan Desai knew that speculation about the moment would be inevitable' (Haham 2006: 51).

Desai also changed the end of the story, convinced he could no longer present the on-screen death of the star: 'He could imagine them cornering him with, "Uncle, we prayed and Amitabh Bachchan lived and now you have killed him"' (ibid: 52). Instead a coda was added, showing Hindus, Muslims, Christians, and Sikhs praying for the hero Iqbal's life, just as they had in reality. Iqbal makes a 'miraculous' recovery, just like the star. The final scene shows Bachchan walking onto a balcony below which is a sign, 'St Philomena's Hospital', a reference to the hospital in Bangalore where the star had initially been treated. He wears symbols of the country's four major religions around his neck and thanks the cheering throngs for their prayers. In real life too, Bachchan 'prayed at each of the centres of worship, giving thanks to all those whose prayers had, it seemed, reached their destinations' (ibid: 152).

Decline and fall of the hero

Coolie was the apogee of Bachchan's stardom, and although he continues to star in films to date, the national hysteria has yet to be replicated. Although Bachchan churned out multiple, commercially successfully releases every year including *Mahaan* (The Great, 1983), *Pukar* (The Call, 1983), and *Sharaabi* (The Drunkard, 1984), and *Mard* (Man, 1985), he was slowing down. Like *Coolie*, these films were star vehicles, recycling 'clapworthy' moments from his earlier hits in crowd-pleasing assemblages and often the star seems to sleepwalk through them, relying on his star status to support increasingly ludicrous on-screen narratives.

However, the biggest factor in Bachchan's change in fortunes was his decision to contest elections from Allahabad, in 1984, following the assassination of Indira Gandhi. His campaign drew on his regional fandom, family legacy, and his closeness to the Gandhi family, and he won by a huge margin.[28] Pritish Nandy credits Bachchan's star persona for his electoral success:

> He was such a big star only because he was the Angry Young Man who could stand up to the might of the brute, ugly political system. Every young person in India identified with him and the roles he played, fighting what you could describe as an almost epic battle against the forces of evil and corruption. He was the hope of the common man, the fire that kept the nation alive during some of its worst years (in Chandra 2006: unpaginated).

However, in 1987, apparently disillusioned and trapped in the growing public storm around the Bofors scandal, Bachchan resigned from parliament to 'return' to cinema.[29] Rumours were rife that the Swedish arms company Bofors had bribed Indian politicians, including the prime minister, Rajiv Gandhi, to ensure the acquisition of their guns by the army. Although Bachchan had held no cabinet position or had obvious direct involvement with the decisions of the cabinet, his personal – and family – proximity to the Gandhi family tainted his image and reception. In 1987, a forged letter directly linked Bachchan and his younger brother, Ajitabh to the scandal. Although both Bachchans and Gandhi denied allegations of bribery, the damage had been done. Gandhi would lose the 1989 elections, partially as a result of the Bofors scandal, while Bachchan would be investigated repeatedly by the incoming government of V.P. Singh.

Of course, throughout his two years in parliament his film releases were still successful, although received with decreasing levels of excitement. In retrospect, *Inquilaab*'s (Uprising, 1984) tale of a small-time vendor's rise, first into the ranks of the police, and then into politics, with the help of a scheming politician seems prescient. The film echoes Bachchan's earlier narratives of the average man making good, but also serves as a grim warning that his 'success' is merely a result of the machinations of more powerful men. The film climaxes with the disillusioned hero massacring corrupt politicians. However, 'unlike Bombay Cinema, India politics cannot be cleaned overnight through the intercession of the angst-ridden modern epic hero' (Mishra 2002: 144). It may well have been Bachchan's star text as the quintessential outsider that hampered his stint in politics as, despite electing him, his fans could not accept their hero joining forces with the very state that excluded them (see Vachani 1999).

His departure from politics was less than easy and he spent the next years suing multiple publications for libel, including Sweden's *Dagens Nyheter* and the USA's diaspora publication, *India Abroad*.[30] He also reached out to the press that he had shunned previously, meeting with key film and mainstream journalists to present his side of the story. However, legal battles were easier to fight than the tide of public opinion that had turned, almost entirely, on their hero and between '1988 and 1990 almost all of Bachchan's films flopped at the box office' (Mishra 2002: 145). Perhaps the dissonance between real-life allegations of bribery and on-screen narrative of the lone force against corruption was too much to bridge even by Bachchan's towering star persona. Moreover, these films were often hasty and clumsy reiterations and copies of his earlier work, and few Bachchan films from 1988 to 2000 broke new ground in narrative, technological or stylistic terms. And yet as he appeared onscreen – in ever more embarrassing films – with clockwork regularity, Bachchan seemed intent on imploding as a star in full view of his public.

At the same time, film narratives were quietly switching to a different genre as romance regained ground with a new generation of fresh-faced leading men. While a middle-aged Bachchan battled the Bofors taint, Aamir Khan debuted with the Romeo-and-Juliet inspired *Qayamat Se Qayamat Tak* (From Apocalypse, Until Apocalypse, 1988) and Salman Khan had early success with *Maine Pyar Kiya* (Yes, I've Fallen in Love, 1989). Both actors are scions of powerful film families and the films seemed to augur the end of the angry young man. The two were soon joined by Shah Rukh Khan, whose own star persona and text would draw upon, imitate, subvert, and contradict Bachchan's.[31]

His on-screen failures led Bachchan to explore other media, including live performances.

> In May 1990, he performed at the Giants Stadium in New Jersey to a packed audience of forty five thousand, and four months later, in September, he made a spectacular entry on a white horse for a performance ("Jumma Chumma in London") at Wembley Stadium (Mishra 2002: 146).

While these performances built on other 'concerts' taken up by the film industry to capitalise on Hindi cinema's diaspora fans, Bachchan's participation marked an early attempt to revive his relationship with his audience, even if that meant shedding some of his aloof demeanour. It also set a precedent that would be exploited with much success by the next generation, who use these live performances to simultaneously elaborate their star personas while offering the illusion of personally relating with fans.[32]

The commercial failure of successive Bachchan films during the Bofors years seemed to induce a sort of amnesia in the press. The moderate success of *Aaj ka Arjun* (Today's Arjun, 1990) paved the way for the press to declare *Hum* (1991) his 'comeback' film. However, much had changed even in that brief, tumultuous period, for Bachchan and for India, including the assassination of Rajiv Gandhi in May 1991, followed by the formation of a Congress-led minority government at the centre. As is often the case in Indian politics, with ouster of V.P. Singh as prime minister and the return of the Congress party, various Bofors- linked cases and inquiries were quietly dropped by the new government.

The 1990s saw regular, albeit fewer, Bachchan releases although most sank without a trace. At least part of the problem was the change brought in by the liberalisation policy embarked upon from 1992 when faced with the threat of fiscal collapse and the possibility of defaulting on World Bank loans, which included wide-ranging economic reforms. As several major industries were deregulated and international corporations granted entry to the Indian market, the country was transformed – seemingly overnight – by the arrival of satellite television. 'As India's growth rate rose beyond 7 percent in the 1990s, the middle classes with their increased spending power came to the forefront' (Chopra 2007: 13). Rebellion, the key aspect of the star's earlier persona, seemed not only hypocritical and out of place for a star tainted by accusations of political corruption, but an anachronism in an age of consumerist aspiration.

Perhaps wanting to participate in the country's rapid changes, in 1995, Bachchan announced the formation of the Amitabh Bachchan Corporation Limited (henceforth ABCL), an ambitious conglomeration of event management and film production, intending to transform the very nature of film-making in the country: 'ABCL tried to organise legitimate finance for the industry. It also tried to finance new kinds of projects' (Dasgupta 2006: 114). ABCL's ambitions were closely linked to Bachchan's own experience and ideas of cinema and, given his own long running difficulties with the press, he 'visualised a wing that would manage celebrity images and careers' (ibid: 114). In its first year, the company posted a turnover of sixty crore rupees and even a profit of fifteen crore rupees.

The company also received the contract for organising the Miss World pageant in Bangalore in 1996, no doubt because of Bachchan's stature. The star linked the event explicitly to the new post-liberalisation narrative: 'I wanted to prove that an Indian show can be a world class event… I've heard so many people treating India as a backward country that I wanted to prove them wrong…' (cited in Oza 2012: 86). However, the pageant soon ran into political opposition and although it was finally held without a glitch, it left ABCL with significant liabilities.

By 1999, ABCL had sought protection under bankruptcy laws.[33] While Bachchan blamed the management, many in the corporate sector believed that the company had spread itself too thin. Bachchan was also still tainted by the Bofors scandal and multiple government investigations, including one for tax evasion. Unsurprisingly, rumours surfaced that the star had 'merely used the corporation to siphon off the equity his company acquired into his personal wealth' (Dasgupta 2006: 116). Whatever the truth, Bachchan was left in 1999 with seemingly insurmountable debts, a dead-end film career, and apparently no way forward.

The star rises again

Despite the failure of ABCL as a business entity, there were good ideas embedded in its ambitions. In the next three years, the government – led by Atal Bihari Vajpayee – would offer a series of incentives and reforms to the film business, including granting it 'industry status'.[34] The new status meant that the 'film industry would finally be eligible for the infrastructural and credit support given to other industries' (Mehta 2005: 136). Other steps soon followed, including 'reduction in custom duties in cinematographic film, exemption of recorded audio and video cassettes from excise duties, and tax incentives' (ibid: 136). Changes also affected the film-making process, driven by technology, globalisation, and the access to extra funding. By the late 1990s, younger stars including Shah Rukh Khan and Aamir Khan were setting up multimedia platforms to make films and expanding to incorporate a host of other media and entertainment activities.

At the same time, as globalisation and its corollary cultural transformations spread across political, social, and economic arenas, the country was also asking itself: 'What does it mean to be Indian?' (Chopra 2007: 14). The answer, ironically, and perhaps unexpectedly, came in the form of the ageing and financially distressed Bachchan. The star recounts the period in his usual life-as-film terms:

> One day, I got up early in the morning and went directly to Yash Chopraji and told him that I was bankrupt. I had no films. My house and a small property in New Delhi were attached. Yashji listened coolly and then offered me a role in his film *Mohabattein*… I then started doing commercials, television and films. And I am happy to say today that I have repaid my entire debt… and am starting afresh (quoted by Ashraf 2003).

The reality is more complicated, including a political subplot of Bachchan's growing distance from the Gandhi family after Rajiv's assassination, not in the least because the Congress party under Sonia – Rajiv's widow – evolved into a beast quite different from the one that the star had known. At the same time, Mandal agitation of the late 1980s, the rise of Hindutva in the early 1990s and globalisation had significantly altered the political and economic landscape of India. Among a clutch of new politically aligned 'industrialists' were Amar Singh, also a political fixer for the Samajwadi Party in Uttar Pradesh at the time, and Sahara group's Subarta Roy. Bachchan would tap into a new combination of political influence and money in exchange for his star value to recover from ABCL's financial debacle.[35]

At the same time as the nation embarked on a consumerist, aspirational path, television graduated from offering government-produced and - sanctioned staid programming for a few hours a day to a dizzy array of twenty-four hour global programming. This exponential television growth went hand in hand with an explosion of the consumer market, with a range of new domestic and international brands that needed advertising. Despite ABCL's failure, the venture had helped 'Bachchan's real-life reinvention as a sleek entertainment entrepreneur…(that)… drew upon the rebellious resourcefulness of his erstwhile screen persona, now tempered by a certain paternal urbanity' (Mazzarella 2003: 158). Elements of his earlier star persona including 'native wit and aggressive individualism' were now harnessed in service of a 'new' India where self-belief and hard-work could lead to material success. Moreover, 'Bachchan was a thoroughly Indian hero' and featuring him allowed brands to address 'the persistent narrative comparing substandard Indian against superior foreign products' (Oza 2012: 129). The deliberate linking of the advertisements between nationalism and nationally produced goods helped counter the postcolonial anxieties of a nation ready to assert itself in the global arena, and Bachchan's star narrative of the scrappy underdog-made-good was ideal for it.

Even the star's membership of the country's educated, politically, and economically powerful elite now became a selling point.[36] 'In the words of one EMW executive: 'We used Amitabh Bachchan as an icon to say that we are not shy of our Indian origin and take pride in being a global Indian citizen' (Mazzarella 2003: 158). Unsurprisingly, the taint of Bofors would

Mohabbatein (2000)

recede from public memory, especially for the new consumers of the increasingly affluent middle class and the star could now vouchsafe the official stamp of approval for a 'whole-hearted embrace of consumerist aspirations' (Mitra 2012: 570).

If the return of the superstar was paved by his appearances in print and television advertisements, it was sealed in 2000 with two key on-screen appearances. The first was a successful return to the big screen as the ageing, iron-willed patriarch in *Mohabbatein*. As the disciplinarian headmaster of a boys' school, Bachchan acted and appeared his age, with grey hair and full beard. Dressed starkly, albeit appropriately for his age, Bachchan reverted to the restrained immobility of his early years, eschewing the familiar, larger-than-life on-screen mannerisms that he had acquired at the peak of his stardom. As Chute points out, 'it actually works for the movie that Bachchan looks like a strange visitor from another era, the *ne plus ultra* of all stern father figures his Vijay characters rebelled against in the Seventies' (2005). The film marked a new phase of Bachchan's on-screen persona, one that drew on his earlier performances and star text, but gave him the gravitas and authority that came with age. It is a persona that he continues to deploy, subvert, and extend to date.[37]

However the full force of Bachchan's comeback was not on the big screen. Instead, the star decided to extend his persona to the small screen, exploiting the country's booming television industry, to appear as the host of India's version of *Who Wants to Be a Millionaire* (*KBC*). This time it was the show's producer who reverted to filmic tropes to describe the gameshow: 'It is not just another quiz game. It's really about human drama. About hope and disappointment' (Siddharth Basu, quoted in Mitra 2012: 571). Within weeks, the show had gained extraordinary popularity, with first-season TRP ratings of 14 while other shows remained in single digits. In subsequent seasons, *KBC*'s ratings would drop to 10.2 although viewer interest remained high and 'STAR TV continued to receive around two hundred thousand calls a day from potential contestants' (Kumar 2005: 329).

Unlike its overseas versions, *KBC* capitalised on Bachchan's star persona, with moments where he repeated well-loved lines from his films and an opening sequence that could only be described as a sermon to the nation. So popular was this 'sermon' that after the initial euphoria subsided, audiences would tune into watch the opening sequence and then tune out again.[38] As Mitra explains,

> On television, Bachchan appeared older and wiser, with a natty beard and a banker's suit. And to its delight, India found that the brooding action man of the 1970s was now sophisticated, self-deprecating and witty, exuding comfortable prosperity rather than rebellion. Just what was needed at a time when India was dreaming about getting rich (2012: 574).

In many ways, *Mohabbatein* and *KBC* bridged the gap between Bachchan's life, screen persona and star text. His prosperity and urbanity no longer destabilized his star text as the rebel. In real life, too, Bachchan seemed to stop fighting his material

Sharing the screen again with wife Jaya in *Kabhi Khushi Kabhie Gham*... (2002)

advantages, picking roles that draw on the earlier angry young man but did not position him in opposition to who he is: a grandfather, an intrinsic part of the country's rich and powerful elite, and the longest enduring star on screen. He has also broadened the range of platforms to engage with his fans, capitalising on new technologies to enhance his star status, with a blog, Facebook page, and an active Twitter account to inform, enhance, and extend his star text.

On a personal level too, Bachchan's earlier conservative star biography of familial stability has been reinforced. He appeared, again after a gap of nearly twenty years, with his wife, Bhaduri, in *Kabhi Khushi Kabhie Gham* (Sometimes Happiness, Sometimes Sorrow, 2001), and has acted with his son, Abhishek, and his daughter-in-law, Aishwarya Rai, in multiple films. Together the four actors have created a formidable 'brand' that extends from film and television to advertising and live shows. The family has also maintained its political presence, albeit with the Samajwadi Party, with Bhaduri elected to India's parliamentary upper house. Old ties to Bollywood royalty, the Kapoors, have been sealed with daughter Shweta's marriage to Nikhil Nanda, the grandson of the legendary Raj Kapoor, and a scion of the powerful Nanda industrialist family.

Since 1969, Bachchan has grown, and then aged, before the nation's eyes. In his on-screen struggles as well as off-screen endurance, India seems to find both familiar comfort and inspiration. Just before his fifty-fifth birthday, Bachchan told veteran journalism Khaled Mohamed that he would keep acting, 'As long as my face and body are acceptable ... the day they aren't, I'll stop' (Mohamed 1997). Nearly two decades later, the superstar appears no closer to such a day.

3 A STAR GREATER THAN THE INDUSTRY

If stars 'matter because they act out aspects of life that matter to us; and performers get to be stars when what they act out matters to enough people' (Dyer 1986: 19), all that Amitabh Bachchan has been acting out matters a great deal to millions of people. In this case, it is necessary to identify these aspects and examine how a single star can act them out over four decades and despite numerous social, political, economic, and cultural transformations. Bachchan's longevity poses a particularly unique dilemma for star studies, given that stars.

> of a given historical period or moment capture their era for us in a range of ways: that the preoccupations, values, conflicts and contradictions of a particular culture, its "climate of feeling", are vividly expressed through its celebrities (Gaffney and Holmes 2007: 1).

In contrast, Bachchan captures not one, but multiple eras, including the social upheaval of the 1970s, the political tumult of the 1980s, the globalisation of the 1990s, and the neo-liberal individualist consumerism of the 2000s. Moreover, given the sheer number and range of his films, the question arises: what do Bachchan's films convey, and, indeed, how do they give expression to a nation experiencing rapid transformation?

This chapter analyses how Bachchan's films engage and interact with a number of national developments and capture the zeitgeist at multiple historic political moments. Although films are rarely intended to coincide with a moment of historical import, their reception – enthusiastic or tepid – can provide insights into a culture at that particular time.[1] Examining the development of Bachchan's star text in reference to a series of key films, released at especially complex historical instances in India can suggest ways in which these filmic texts reflected, refracted, and resonated with, the nation's preoccupations. Such scrutiny can indicate ways in which Bachchan's stardom may be read as 'a symbolic portal into the nature of a culture' with 'stars as that culture's ultimate expression' (Gaffney and Holmes 2007: 1).

A new screen for a new kind of star

Bachchan's entry into cinema can be traced to the global and national economic changes of the 1950s and 1960s. Newly independent India's 'industrial power' model coincided with changes in Western economies, especially that of the US, and the 'increased pressure from lower cost exports from developing countries' (Vitali 2008: 193).[2] European economies were feeling similar pressures on their manufacturing sectors, a corollary of decolonisation. In India, the economy had grown significantly but the centralised economic planning policies were increasingly seen as hindrances. Faced with demands for liberalisation, the government initially embarked on a series of measures to deregulate state controls on the market. However, successive droughts in 1965 and 1966 left India at the mercy of food aid from the US, which used these measures to push through the World Bank's policy demands. These policies would be reversed by Indira Gandhi, beginning in 1970. The pressures of the Cold War, as well as decolonisation narratives also played a part, as the US was reconfigured in the national imaginary as a 'new coloniser'.[3]

As the state expanded its policy of economic centralisation, including taking full control of rupee capital flow and centralising credit, the country's 'black market' grew exponentially.[4] At the same time, labour policies failed to keep up with the wider programme, and the concurrent shrinking of the manufacturing sector led to increased unemployment. The ranks of the unemployed and disillusioned had also been swelled by the decline of the country's agricultural sector, not only because of the famines, but also due to a gradual transition from a feudal-agrarian economy to the initial semblance of a market economy.

Gandhi's policies seem particularly wrong-headed given that they coincided with the coming-of-age of the first post-independence generation, who had benefited from the expansion of the education sector under Jawaharlal Nehru's ambitious modernisation programmes. This growing mass of educated and unemployed young people joined the large unemployed proletariat at the same time as the state actively restricted economic growth.[5] Indeed, 'never before the 1970s had the occupation of the characters been so prominent a concern in Hindi films' (Vitali 2008: 215) as cinema attempted to reflect the key concern of the times.[6]

Some albeit not many of Bachchan's early films reflect this wider context: *Pyar ki Kahani* (Story of Love, 1971) features him as an overqualified young man unable to secure better employment while *Raaste ka Patthar* (The Obstacle, 1972) sees him as a bachelor who allows his superiors at work use of his flat for sexual adventures, emphasising the precarious status of the newly constituted professional classes.[7]

However these markers of the urban middle class form one of the two entry points for the construction of his star text and initially Bachchan found a 'hospitable climate' in 'middle-class' cinema. It is interesting to note that the middle-class persona Bachchan projected in most of these films did not portray the class anxieties – including secure employment – that seemed to grip the nation. These were comfortable characters, maintaining the status quo in their middle-class trappings, and although they may have aspired to love, or have been thwarted by familial obligations, their socio-economic status was fully secured. Indeed, the idea of economic worry is missing from most of Bachchan's early films, including *Parwaana* and *Ek Nazar*. In a country gripped by overwhelming economic disquiet, few opportunities and a seemingly all-powerful state, this persona did not capture the zeitgeist of the nation nearly as effectively as the angry young man soon would.

Although the internal division, political instability and economic despair of the post-independence generation that was coming of age made for a potent brew, it still hadn't reached the critical mass required to produce a new form of expression. This was provided by the 1971 war with Pakistan, an event whose impact on the Indian popular imagination has yet to be considered fully. Independent India had been fully committed to Gandhian non-violence, even establishing it as a principle of its foreign policy under Nehru. However, the 1962 Sino-Indian war came as a shock to the Indian political and military establishment. Chinese support for Pakistan during the 1965 war further exacerbated India's regional anxieties, leading it further into the Soviet camp during the Cold War (also a factor in the economic decisions discussed earlier). After the Chinese nuclear tests in 1964, India accelerated its own nuclear programme, and finally the 1971 war decisively marked the end of non-violence as state policy and ideology.

Of all the military actions undertaken by India since independence, 1971 is most clearly one of choice albeit with sound strategic military and political rationale. It also provided India with its first convincing military victory. The Indo-Soviet Treaty of Friendship signed in August 1971 helped Gandhi openly challenge the US, signalling the arrival of a new, postcolonial, and aggressive India. Pakistan's surrender on 16 December 1971, and the transformation of East Pakistan

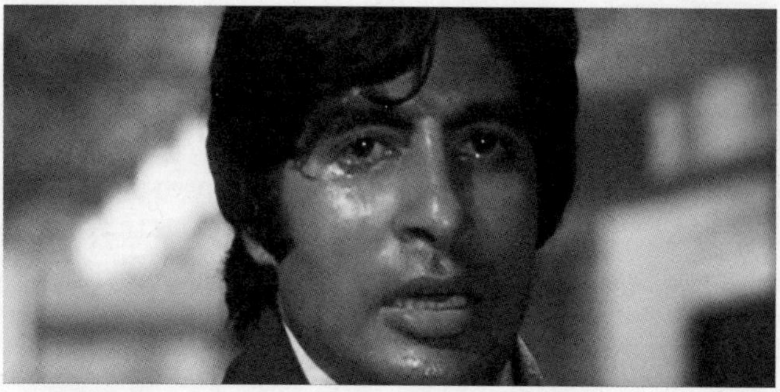

Zanjeer (1973)

into the independent nation-state of Bangladesh informed a new narrative, that violence could not only achieve 'just' and moral ends but that aggression was in fact a suitable way forward, delivering not only justice but victory. India's first round of nuclear tests on 18 May 1974 further sealed the narrative of an assertive nation-state not only willing but also able to deploy violence when required.[8] Moreover, although rejection by the global 'nuclear club,' placed India on the margins of international law, the government asserted its decision in 'moral' rather than 'legal' terms. The country would continue to emphasise its right to a 'peaceful' nuclear programme, positioning itself as a moral, albeit weaker member of a global system dominated by an elite club of nations.[9]

This new aggression found its perfect on-screen embodiment in the 'angry young man'. Beginning with *Zanjeer*, Bachchan's film persona drew on the nation's frustrations and anxieties but resolved them with a brooding anger punctuated by explosive violence. *Zanjeer*'s Vijay is an honest police officer who often relies on extra-judicial methods to pursue justice. Even though the film is often described as a 'revenge' narrative, Vijay does not seek personal revenge; indeed, he has no memory of his parents' murder or the killer. It is only as part of his larger quest for justice that he runs into the killer, Teja (Ajit). It is the fact that Teja's life of crime continues that provides the moral justification for Vijay's actions. Moreover, in the film, 'vengeance carried a quasi-revolutionary fervour (public revenge) that is also directly linked to a private trauma' (Mishra 2002: 134). It may even be argued that Vijay's location as the hero who simultaneously represents the state as well as being outside the law is what caught the nation's imagination: 'It is the act of switching sides, positioning himself on the side of the 'illegal' (but morally upright) margin, that gives the figure its power' (Prasad 1998: 144).

The movie not only articulated the personal as political, but also provided a vehicle for the anger of a post-colonial generation that felt denied the fruits promised by independence: 'the rags-to-riches theme that always paralleled the narrative of personal revenge in Bachchan's films was the imaginary fulfilment of the slum dweller's own fantasies' (Mishra 2002: 128). At the same time, academic formulations of Bachchan's initial star persona as one principally, if not entirely, derived from the socially, politically, and economically marginalised have turned into orthodoxy. Even in 2011, Ghosh asserts that the star's 'image became a technology for imaging anti-establishmentarian desires, especially on the part of those who felt left out of the electoral calculus' (2011: 169). Such a construction ignores both the rapid socio-political transformations of the 1970s and 1980s as well as the star's cross-class appeal, specifically because of the contradictions between his biography and screen persona. Rather than embodying 'rogue masculinities– the outlaw, the outsider – at a time when to be an outsider posed considerable political risks' (Banerjea 2005: 166), Bachchan's personal biography legitimised him for the 'aspirational' classes by locating him in the country's entrenched elite.

Moreover, this 'anger' of the era was not necessarily that of the 'lumpen proletarian', or the millions of poor in the slums.

The anger was multi-dimensional, a judgement that man is faced with in the new age, a despair at the lack of institutional responsiveness to problems, and the need to release the necessary energy required to act single-handedly on behalf of the system (Dasgupta 2006: 15).

Bachchan himself formulates this anger as legitimate – especially for the middle classes, claiming that he draws his 'anger' from his father's writings. The angry young man may have been raging but he was also deeply conservative, seeking to reform rather than destroy his host environment. His anger was righteous and his violence was at the service of his society, and of the nation-state; India's first post-independence hero was not renouncing, but reaffirming nationalist dreams.

Over the next two years, this persona would begin to confront an unjust state as well, 'fighting for righteous causes from outside its sphere of operation', but there is never any 'doubt that he is on the side of Right' (Dwyer and Patel 2002: 35). Javed Akhtar explains the growth of this screen persona:

He wages war against the injustice he had to endure and he emerges the winner. You can see that the hero who had developed between 1973 and 75 – the Emergency was declared in India in 1975 – reflected those times (quoted in Dwyer and Patel 2002: 35).

Deewar's Vijay also reflects the increasing urbanisation of the country, as youth from the rural hinterlands moved to urban centres, driven by a combination of aspirations and the rapid breakdown of the agrarian, feudal economy. In the city, they faced desperate need and cruelty, accompanied by the daily, banal humiliations of urban, anonymous poverty. Indeed the 'migration of destitute villagers into cities and towns' was unprecedented and contributed to 'the mushrooming of slums' that would increasingly become the backdrop for the 'angry young man's' fury (Kazmi 1998). *Deewar* repeatedly refers to incidents in

Vijay's childhood that explain his actions as an adult, clearly locating his rage and aggression in the initial brutal expulsion of the family and the humiliations that the city heaps upon its poor. Prasad points to the 'double identity' that marks Bachchan's persona at this stage, split between the 'proletarian hero' and the representative of the state (1998: 144).

Deewar also juxtaposes the righteously angry young man operating outside the confines of the law with the middle-class professional who wants to reassert the 'values' of the state and society. Vijay's younger brother Ravi (Shashi Kapoor) embodies the latter, his rise from the 'footpath' to a police officer signalling professional aspirations of the country's youth while also affirming the conservative values that privilege gradual 'legal' change over the tumult of illegal albeit moral revolution. Not surprisingly, even as Bachchan's narratives from this point forward focus on the angry young man's ire, they also reinforce the state's primacy because 'his lawlessness' has to be punished and his character must die at the end of the film (Dwyer 2000: 124).

Deewar's success has often been attributed to a hero 'who not only emerged from the working class, but whose silence and suppressed rage lent a voice to the angst of the urban poor' (Kazmi 1998: 124). Such a reading over-emphasises a simplistic construction of class which ignores the ways the film deploys Bachchan's sophisticated, elite persona to address the aspirations of a growing, urban, young middle class.[10] While Ravi continues to inhabit materially spare spaces as a member of the law-abiding (and -enforcing) middle class, Vijay's illegal activities deliver the kind of material excess that seemed fantastic to most Indians in the 1970s. Moreover, Bachchan's physicality and costuming are used to signal that he is 'at home' with his newly acquired wealth. Unlike the crass nouveau riche clothing of the gangsters – including a memorable leopard jacket – Vijay's clothes are quietly fashionable, demonstrating his ease with the trappings of success. His body language is comfortable, cocky even, despite

With Parveen Babi in *Deewar* (1975)

his dockworker's uniform in Davar's (Iftekhar) office. At a later meeting with Davar by the pool of a five-star hotel, his beige flares and matching tweed jacket are in stark contrast to the louder clothes of the rest of the gangsters[11] and his lounging posture conveys his familiarity with the luxurious surroundings, compared to those around him. His wealth is indicated by a pair of Aviator sunglasses, an early nod to international cosmopolitanism that was still unusual in a film industry – and society – that struggled to combine material wealth with the subtler markers of 'class'.

If the film spectator, as the 'consumer of the star image brings his or her own hopes, desires and dreams to the encounter, and plays an active role in selecting which aspects of the star matter' (Gaffney and Holmes 2007: 9), then Vijay's ease with wealth provides a locus of desire for the middle classes who aspired to not only wealth but also the intangible markers of success. While scholars have explored the contradictions of Bachchan's biography and screen persona as a point of destabilisation, these same aspects allowed him to straddle class divides, and expanded his appeal as a star. Thus, the 'de-classing' of the angry young man in filmic narratives by social, economic, and geographical dislocations helps him 'address the crisis of the period as a figure representing the margins of society' (Mazumdar 2007: 8). At the same time, Bachchan's personal class location enabled him to address spectators who were not at the margins but who aspired to enhanced socio-economic status.

Rage recedes before the state

Deewar's Vijay seems to be the last time that Hindi cinema would mount a clear challenge to the state although the persona would linger and inform Bachchan's roles for most of the next decade. After *Deewar*, the angry young man would subtly change both the object of his rage and its causes. In *Trishul*, his fury would be motivated by personal revenge; in *Kaala Patthar*, by an earlier disappointment in himself; in *Muqaddar ka Sikandar*, the anger is even more diffuse, more of an excuse for a self-absorbed hero who seems to be another avatar of the self-destructive Devdas, thwarted by social mores and seeking an idealised lost love; in *Lawaaris* (Illegitimate, 1981), the indignation seems even more entitled, that of an illegitimate child denied access to material wealth with its corollary of idealised maternal love and emotional security. As such, *Deewar* is distinct from other Bachchan films 'in that the protagonist's anger is directed against a generalised power network unleashing everyday humiliation against the disenfranchised millions' (Virdi 2008: 230). In all the other films, even if a generalised 'system' is evoked in speech, the protagonist's struggle remains against another *individual*, generally a politician or industrialist, and never against the full might of the nation-state.

The shift from the moral hero raging against the injustice of the system seen in *Deewar* – released in late January 1975 – is sudden, happening in the same year, and marked by the

Emergency, and the release of *Sholay*. The Emergency was an attempt by Mrs Gandhi to calm the social and labour unrest threatening to overwhelm her government. Political opposition to her policies was coalescing under Jayaprakash Narayan's call for '*Sampoorna Kranti*' (Total Revolution) against 'corruption and misgovernment and black marketing, profiteering and hoarding, to fight for the overhaul of the educational system and for a real people's democracy' (quoted in Bhattacharjea 2004: 205–6). On 8 May 1974, the All-India Railwaymen's Federation, led by George Fernandes, declared a nation-wide strike, crippling the transport services. The railways were joined by other trade and student unions and political parties joined in:

> There were demonstrations; strikes; fasts, often "unto death"; *bandhs*, or general strikes; *gheraos*, or virtual imprisonment of authorities by picketing their offices and prohibiting their exits; *dharnas*, or agitations at the premises of the institutions being protested (Tharoor 1998: 211).

According to one estimate, 'as much as 47 percent of the organised labour force in 1974 may have been involved in some strike action' (quoted in Lal 2011: 23). These combined movements mounted a 'concentrated assault' on the 'existing structures of class and caste' that had benefited till then from the 'state's collusion' (Jain 2007: 338). However the narrative for the nation's elite was that the Emergency was 'an attempt to instil order in an unruly society' (ibid: 19).

The resentment people felt against the state formed the backdrop for the production of *Sholay* that began in 1973 and informs the deeply conservative nature of the film. Perhaps the better-known trivia is that the Emergency required the film's producers to substantially alter the original ending in order to reinforce the supremacy of the state with the police arriving to arrest the villain.[12] However, regardless of the altered ending, *Sholay*[13] marks a departure from the 'angry young man' of *Zanjeer* and *Deewar*, even though the three films are often analysed together.

Again scripted by Salim-Javed, the film attributes the anger to the villain, Gabbar Singh (Amjad Khan), a brutal and psychopathic dacoit. Bachchan's character Jai and his friend Veeru (Dharmendra) are hired by the local landlord, Thakur (Sanjeev Kumar), a former policeman, to capture Gabbar. By representing Thakur as the wronged party, the audience is 'seduced into participating in a reaffirmation of the feudal order' (Prasad 1998: 155). That Thakur is also a former policeman helps to confirm the links between the older feudal order and the modern nation-state. In contrast, Gabbar, with his hideout in the wilderness and coarse language, is the rural rebel reconfigured as a brutal outlaw.

Given the Indian state's continuing crackdown on peasant revolts, especially the Naxalite movement, as well as its struggle against the 'dacoits' in deeply impoverished parts of rural India, such as the Chambal, this narrative reconfiguration marks a significant departure for Salim-Javed and Bachchan. In *Sholay*, even though Jai and Veeru act to reinforce the will of a conservative social order, their identification as petty criminals sets them up as 'infra-legal, but not irredeemably criminal, figures with whom the new proletarian and other disaffected audiences could identify' (ibid: 155). Here it is interesting that while both Jai and Veeru are nominally de-classed, their outfits and attitudes locate them as urban, albeit itinerant, figures.

Moreover, Jai's language, mannerisms, and a social confidence that traverses class – such as when Veeru sends him to Basanti's (Hema Malini) aunt with his marriage proposal – are subtle signals of his higher social class (and caste). Jai's aspirations – and morality – are also constituted as those of a modern man:[14] unlike Veeru, he falls in love with Thakur's widowed daughter-in-law Radha (Jaya Bhaduri), and even receives Thakur's tacit approval for the match. Although Jai's courtship is discreet, there is no indication that he doubts his ability to woo Radha, nor any concern that a mere 'petty

Superstar of the multi-star blockbuster. *Sholay* (1975)

criminal' may not be acceptable to her or Thakur. Furthermore, despite his ostensibly egalitarian friendship with Veeru, he has the final word on the decisions the duo make, either by insisting his idea is 'reasonable' or by tricking the gullible Veeru with his 'lucky' coin. As such, Jai's role as the enforcer of the feudal order and the state and his violence against the agrarian subaltern challenger place him squarely on the side of the entrenched elite.

Given Bachchan's real-life – and well-publicised – proximity to the Gandhi family, the film may also be read as a reiteration of conservative socio-political values that, instead of forming a high point of the 'aesthetic of mobilisation',[15] marks the end of the angry young man. After *Sholay*, Bachchan would continue to play the urban proletarian – mineworker, coolie, petty crook –with the ability and willingness to use violence to achieve his own ends, but he would no longer rage to reform an unjust social political order. Seen in this light, Bachchan's own 'reformulation of the source of this anger in markedly bourgeois (and generic terms)', takes on greater significance (Mishra 2002: 128).

The conservative impulse of *Sholay* that dampens the angry young man's rage also opens new avenues for the star. Jai is 'not weighed down by sorrow' nor is he 'tormented by a superior conception that promises a better world' (Dasgupta 2006: 32). Instead, he displays vulnerability and emotion, even if he's reluctant to reveal them. And this vulnerability allows him the possibility of a love interest, absent from his previous films: in *Zanjeer*, Vijay's love life was incidental to his friendship with Sher Khan (Pran); in *Deewar*, Anita serves more as a plot device than any focus of intense love.[16] Even in smaller-budget films like *Majboor* and *Abhimaan*, love works more as a plot device than any overwhelming motivating force for Bachchan's characters. *Sholay* changed that forever: in one of the film's most powerful scenes, Jai sits on the veranda of his cottage, playing the harmonica, and watching as Radha turns off the oil lamps on her balcony. The plaintive notes of his tune fill the physical gap between the two of them as well as highlighting the narrative impossibility of a consummation. Despite Jai's tragic end, the film opened up the possibility of the lover, one that the star would develop in films like *Kabhie Kabhie* and *Kasme Vade* (Sworn Vows, 1978). Even when thwarted in 'true love' as in *Muqaddar ka Sikandar*, the reticent, violent hero would find comfort, affection and devotion from the courtesan, Zohrabai (Rekha), a role that references Chandramukhi from earlier *Devdas* films.[17] In *Kaala Patthar*, the hero's self-recriminations and eventual salvation are accompanied by the discreet, hero-worshipping love of Dr Sudha Sen (Rakhee Gulzar).[18] It is worth noting, however, that Bachchan's romantic appeal despite these roles remains incidental to his screen persona, with the love story forming one of the many attractions in the narrative, generally as an attempt to counter-balance the more dominant attraction of violence.[19] Indeed, by the mid-1980s, Manmohan Desai, who made some of Bachchan's biggest hits, noted that the star lacked 'an out and out romantic image' (quoted in Vachani 1999: 207).

Sholay also gave Bachchan a chance to explore comedy, an aspect that would prove more crucial to his star persona than the

Romance was never a significant aspect of Bachchan's star persona although most films at least had a nominal love story. In *Satte pe Satta* (1982)

notion of romance. Although the film plays Veeru's exuberant slapstick off against Jai's sobriety, it also grants Bachchan's character some notable comic moments. In the much-loved scene when Jai goes to Basanti's aunt to convince her of Veeru's eligibility, his sombre demeanour delivers the comedy. Given the friends' earlier interaction, the audience is left in no doubt that Jai's sabotaged proposal is completely deliberate, and the scene is played entirely for laughs. Moreover, the song 'Yeh dosti', provides an opportunity for joyful capers, a reminder of his light-hearted role in *Bombay to Goa*, prefiguring the physical exuberance that is the hallmark of Anthony Gonsalves of *Amar Akbar Anthony* (1977).

Most importantly, *Sholay* suggests that the reticent, sombre hero could have a hidden playful side which might be revealed in the right circumstances. In a fleeting sequence, Jai runs into Radha in the village. He has been riding a buffalo, and cuts a ludicrous figure. Radha's amusement is contrasted with Jai's immediate and deep embarrassment at having been spotted playing the fool, although his slide off the animal is equally gangly and awkward, heightening Radha's – and the audience's – amusement. This capacity for comedy – even at his own expense – is developed in Bachchan's later films. As the angry young man loses his anger, comedy and romance help expand and extend the range of characters he can play, and the ways in which his star persona can develop.

Superstar of the *Masala* film

After *Sholay*'s phenomenal success, the angry young man's ire was concretised in individual terms, even as he distanced himself from what Rajadhyaksha and Willemen call a 'lumpen rebel-vigilante' (1994: 49). Instead, Bachchan would play a 'larger-than-life hero' who would take on a recognisable enemy: 'The smuggler, the drug baron, the mafia kingpin, the local dada, the scheming industrialist, the unscrupulous rich man' were to blame for the misfortunes of the 'common man' (Kazmi 1996:19). The larger concerns of poverty, unemployment, and structural inequity could all be blamed on an individualised and therefore vanquish-able enemy.

Two major motives emerged for the hero's violence: individualised revenge that would nevertheless wear the cloak of justice; and upward mobility, viewed as righteous necessity because the hero required material means to challenge and defeat his enemy. Yet the hero's means and methods would technically infringe the laws of the state (Vachani 1999), thus harnessing some of the earlier rebellion and cementing the symbolic connection between the star and the nation's disenfranchised. On screen, Bachchan's characters belonged to the same economic class: 'a coolie, a dock worker, a waiter, a tangewala, a cop, a petty crook. In short, always a small-timer who is equally victimized by the bad guys – smugglers, drug pedlars, dacoits, corrupt politicians, mafia hoods and scheming industrialists' (Kazmi 1996: 33).

But the character was also one ready to bend the rules, even benefit a little – if not a lot – from the same system: Vijay of *Hera Pheri* (Scamsters,1976) is a small-time conman; Ahmed of

Imaan Dharam (Faith/Morality, 1977) is paid for false testimony; Sikandar of *Muqaddar ka Sikandar* acquires a fortune by turning in smuggled goods to the police for cash. In using the corrupt, unjust system for his benefit, the post-*Sholay* hero is co-opted by the same system and, for the most part, is happy to accept the rewards of such a relationship.

Indeed, India's post-Emergency history suggests that the 'tough guy' was better suited to the nation's mood than the earlier enraged avatar. Prasad places *Deewar* in a trajectory of films representing the 'consequences of the failure of the legal system of the modern state' (1998: 152) but also notes that, unlike earlier rural dacoits, Bachchan's character doesn't start a gang to battle feudal oppression but 'joins an existing' one instead and 'rises to the top' (ibid: 153). The end of Emergency and the 1977 elections gave India its first non-Congress government, one that had been elected in protest rather than as a real alternative. One of the most emotive issues in an election framed almost entirely around the excesses of the state during the Emergency was the forced sterilisation of poor men in both rural and urban areas. The state's direct assault on proletarian 'masculinity' had been countered by the angry young man, but with Mrs Gandhi's defeat, this anger – at least on screen – became a fading echo of an 'emasculated' rage.

The Janata Party coalition lasted until 1980, proving a pyrrhic victory for those who had hoped that the new dispensation would transform the oppressive, corrupt state, and extending the dominant narrative that, without the active involvement of the nation's elite (especially the Congress party), the country would dissolve into chaos. The return of Mrs Gandhi to power after the election of 1980 sealed the political status quo, and the only way to progress was to 'rise to the top' rather than rage futilely against it.

Although Bachchan's films in this period, continue to highlight the 'fundamental and irreversible separation between the people or nation, whose voice is often represented by the hero's mother, and the nation' (Vitali 2008: 207), conservative values are reaffirmed and his tough guy persona poses no challenge to the primacy of the state. Instead he uses violence as a means to attain his own ends, especially to achieve upward mobility, albeit at the margins of the law. The tough guy's location on the margins of legality is not coincidental as post-1977 India accepts corruption, brutality and crime as endemic to the 'system' and only to be resisted when these become personal.[20]

Unsurprisingly, there are only two narrative options for this tough guy: either victory against all odds in films like *Kaala Patthar* or *Don*, or a glorious death in *Sholay* or *Muqaddar ka Sikandar*, 'adding martyrdom to his cause' (Dwyer and Patel 2002: 35). In the first option, he gains material and emotional rewards, thus validating his anger and violence while in the latter, the star's death becomes part of the spectacle, drawing on his star status to provide the pleasures of tragedy while the narrative reaffirms the primacy of the order he has challenged.

After 1978 and *Muqaddar ka Sikandar*, however, martyrdom is no longer an option for the superstar, perhaps as a corollary of his co-option by the elite order.[21] After this point, Bachchan's characters are pitted against increasingly ludicrous villains – including the Bond-style villain Shakal (Kulbhushan Kharbanda) in *Shaan* (Glory, 1980) and the obsessive Zafar (Amjad Khan) in *Coolie*. Violence becomes another of the attractions[22] of Bachchan's films and star persona, providing an escapist, cathartic release in a period when the country was trapped in growing cycles of dysfunction and violence, including insurgency in Punjab that culminated in the Indian troops' assault on the Golden Temple to clear the militants and in turn directly led to the assassination of Mrs Gandhi in 1984, and the consequent mass slaughter of Sikhs in many cities. It is telling that in *Coolie*, when star text and filmic narrative, star persona and real life collide, and with Bachchan nearly dying during filming, the film must change its conclusion, allowing even the tragic hero to miraculously live. In some ways, *Coolie*'s wish fulfilment takes on additional significance in light of the growing sense of the nation-state's disintegration: the hero must live, if only on screen, to help imagine a nation that can also survive violent dismemberment.

Comforts (or illusion) of hope and the superstar

However, the 'tough guy' persona alone would not be sufficient to maintain stardom or indeed elevate Bachchan to superstar status. Relying solely on a willingness and ability to inflict violence could have reduced him to purely an 'action film' star, much in the mould of Sunil Dutt and Dara Singh before him, or his contemporaries such as Shatrughan Sinha or Vinod Khanna. However, in 1977, a new twist was introduced to Bachchan's screen persona by director Manmohan Desai, which not only extended it and sealed his star status but also made it practically impossible for any of his contemporaries to imitate him.[23]

After *Sholay*, Bachchan's films, to a large extent, became star vehicles, drawing on his 'angry young man' persona, deploying 'narrative, performance sequence and action spectacle' in the manner of a 'cinema of attraction' (Vasudevan 2000). For Bachchan, these included sequences that highlighted his brooding intensity punctuated by bursts of violence, an emotional scene generally involving a mother or paternal figure, a nominal process of recruiting sundry members of the subaltern – a petty criminal, alcoholic, or street urchin – to his cause, and a series of intensifying confrontations with the designated villain and his henchmen. In short, the star would brood, challenge, love, weep and fight, each recognisable sequence building on his earlier performances and providing a replicated, yet novel, spectatorial pleasure.

In contrast to the earlier astutely scripted texts, these films were primarily 'built around the roles, scenes and iconography of the star' and the 'presentation of the star' was 'heightened

Expanding his star persona. As Anthony Gonsalves in *Amar, Akbar, Anthony* (1977)

in powerful dialogues, but most importantly in the film song' (Dwyer 2000: 123) where his appearance was emphasised by the use of dance, costume, and make-up.[24] In some ways, there was no better director to construct star vehicles than Desai 'who subordinated the narrative to these "items" (as he called attractions), piling on item on item' (Dwyer and Patel 2002: 31) with dizzying zeal and extraordinary skill. Although many of Desai's later films would rely almost entirely on star value and an increasingly weary replication of proven set pieces, *Amar Akbar Anthony* reveals a finely tuned ability to string the 'items' or attractions together to create a coherent, if mind-boggling, whole. The film is also crucial to a consideration of Bachchan's stardom as it introduces the element of comedy to the star's repertoire of cinematic 'attractions'.

Desai's films can be seen as the comic flipside of the 'angry young man'. They draw on the same circumstances of poverty and social marginalisation, but offer a heroic catharsis in laughter rather than a depressing reflection of society's deepest wounds. Indeed, it may be argued that Anthony Gonsalves constitutes for the first time in Indian cinema, a figure that embodies writer-director Marcel Pagnol's noble clown: 'But if he must degrade himself and if he consents, his merit is even greater because he sacrifices his pride to lighten our suffering' (quoted in Haham 2006: 110).[25] A great part of the film's spectatorial pleasure is the incongruity of seeing Anthony's lack of dignity contrasted with Bachchan's real-life power and prestige and his earlier brooding, on-screen persona. Yet this contradiction also imbues Anthony with on-screen power and Bachchan's star persona with longevity:

> It is as if the Anthony-Bachchan sandwich had been designed as part of a government Five Year Plan in anticipation of the move to a neo-liberal model of development: a figure who in life represented the aspirations of bourgeois India to realize what market ideology had to offer, and who in film could cathect the experiences of disenfranchised 'heroes' on the street hoping to catch a break (Elison *et al.* 2016: 121–2).

The first confrontation between Amar (Vinod Khanna) and Anthony relies on the director's skilful weaving of a brilliant pastiche soundtrack and a ridiculous fight sequence choreographed to emphasise Bachchan's clownish imitations of Hong Kong martial arts films against Khanna's 'traditional' macho man. The film enables Bachchan to carry the comedy, with the actor parodying his own macho image. Having crashed the Easter party looking for Jenny (Parveen Babi), Anthony is beaten up, partly as a consequence of being drunk. In possibly one of the most beloved sequences of Hindi cinema, he steadies himself in front of the mirror, still reeling, examines his wounds, berating himself for his drunken antics, and tends to his injuries by carefully applying first iodine and then band aid… to the mirror. The sequence topped the list of favourite screen moments for both Desai and Bachchan and marked the birth of another of the star's attractions; after Anthony Gonsalves, the star's films would inevitably include a comic 'drunk' scene although none quite matched up to the hilariously absurd quality of the original.

Yet the song before the drunken sequence, 'My Name Is Anthony Gonsalves', is also crucial to Bachchan's star text, framing the actor – for the first time – in overt terms as an 'item' number, in a song-and-dance sequence that typically focuses on female actors to allow 'heightened transgressive pleasures' (Kasbekar 2001: 293). The song frames the star in similarly sexually pleasurable terms, focusing on Bachchan's physique, costume and antics, displacing the traditionally female object of desire (Jenny, in the song).[26] This centring of the male star as the locus of desiring pleasures also contributed to Bachchan's array of 'attractions'. The song maintains the conventions of the female 'item number', using a bar or nightclub as a setting, with elaborate, even fantastic costumes, but displaces the female body with that of the male star. *Naseeb*'s (Fate, 1981) 'John Johnny Janardan', *Kaalia*'s 'Jahan teri yeh nazar hai', and *Laawaris*'s 'Apni to jaise taise', are just some of the 'item numbers' that followed Anthony's first appearance. *Yaarana* (Friendship, 1981) would in fact locate Bachchan as a pop star, providing multiple and increasingly elaborate song-and-dance numbers to emphasise his centrality to spectatorial desires. In these 'item numbers', as in the films, despite the presence of a glamorous, even scantily clad, woman, it is always Bachchan who occupies centre-screen and is presented as the central object of desire.[27]

These elements of comedy and the positioning of the male body as the focus of the 'item number' became essential aspects of the Hindi film's attractions, and continue to be employed to enhance the screen presence of other male stars. However, no other star has been able to exploit the combination of violence with comedy and sexualisation with quite the same success.[28] These songs also became the hallmarks of what Dasgupta calls the 'epic film' and were intended to make Bachchan's persona 'appear larger and larger' (2006:77). In these films, strong scripts, sharp editing and cinematic techniques gave way to a series of attractions centred around the star, all intended to present him as larger than life as possible. All other elements of cinema were subordinated to 'capturing Amitabh Bachchan as a fresco of all kinds of philosophical and histrionic possibilities' (ibid: 78). The attractions included not only the fight scenes, lavishly filmed songs, and dramatic dialogues, but also the star's emotional and drunk scenes. Indeed, 'this combination of strength and vulnerability partly explained his cultic popularity' (Bhattacharya 2013: 156). Bachchan was often presented in tableaux-like longshots, followed by a zoom to his face (Mazumdar 2000). He was also increasingly backlit for dramatic effect and to heighten his iconic stature. The epic films also mark the introduction of more elaborate and stylised costumes for Bachchan, including the now iconic white suit, a stark visual marker of difference not only from the early proletarian hero but also the 'masses' that adored him.

End of the rage

By the early 1980s, and despite the many social and political changes in the country, Bachchan's screen persona still deployed elements from the previous decade, requiring a forced 'ordinariness' of characters with concurrent themes and a sense of anger, rebellion, and social isolation (Prasad 1998: 141). By the mid-1970s, Bachchan films had bigger budgets, with lavish sets, overseas locales, and high production values (Vitali 2008) and, later in the decade, his star vehicles increasingly removed themselves visually and narratively from their 'putative intended audience' (Bhattacharya 2013: 154).[29] By the early 1980s, Bachchan's screen persona with its link to the 'common man' was becoming destabilised by his off-screen status and material wealth: 'Part of the aura surrounding the Bombay film industry is the wealth amassed by top stars like Bachchan. That these fortunes depend on tax evasion is public knowledge, and

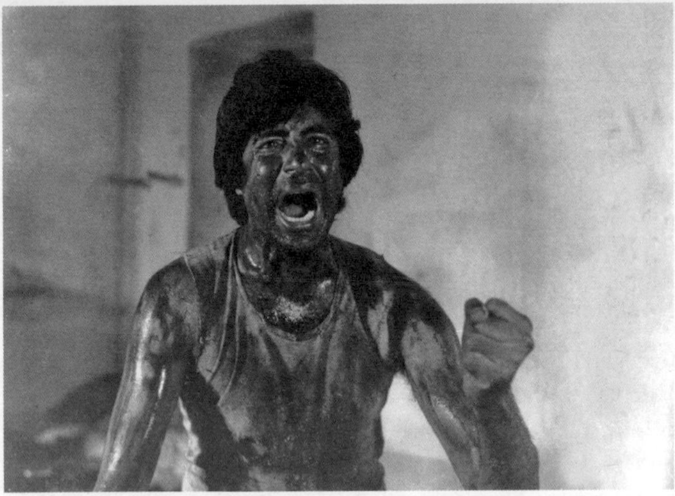

Proletarian as disguise. *Kaala Patthar* (1979)

speculation in the 1980s abounded about Amitabh Bachchan's wealth' (Virdi 2008: 234).

Perhaps the combination of off-screen wealth and rumours of tax evasion would have eventually – inevitably – destabilised both the star's on-screen identification with the urban proletariat and the illegal-but-moral rectitude that marked his rebellion(s). Moreover, by 1984, the regular iterations of Bachchan's 'clap worthy' sequences repackaged in multiple films were beginning to feel stale. Even *Coolie*'s success – the year before – was at least in part due to the extra-filmic near-death of the star.

However, the process was accelerated by the star's decision to enter politics in the aftermath of Mrs Gandhi's assassination in 1984. Vachani (1999) blames Bachchan's image as the 'quintessential outsider' for his eventual failure as a politician but the truth may be more complicated. The star's image relied on his initial roles as the angry young man, and he was positioned by his party – and despite the instabilities caused by his real-life power and wealth – as the 'voice of the people'. Bachchan won the 1984 election by an overwhelming majority, due to a combination of the 'sympathy wave' in favour of the Congress party after Mrs Gandhi's assassination and his own popularity.

Rajiv Gandhi, the heir to the Congress party, was an unknown entity at the time and it was hoped he would usher in a new, less corrupt phase of electoral politics. Called 'Mr Clean', for a record untainted by rumours or charges of corruption, he and his associates were seen as fresh, new faces, and 'there were high hopes for radical change in the nature of national politics' (Virdi 1993: unpaginated). Perhaps this is why the Bofors allegations of bribery and corruption were so damaging for Gandhi and, by extension, for Bachchan. The inconsistencies between Bachchan's screen persona and his role as a member of parliament was fundamentally untenable.[30]

If Bachchan's decline provides an interesting glimpse of the ways star texts embody, represent and interact with national narratives and zeitgeists, then the difficulties he faced

The hero's decline. *Shahenshah* (1988)

in effecting a come-back demonstrate the ways in which India had changed. With the rise of caste-politics, a new generation of urban proletariat and rural subaltern had risen to power; the ascent of politicians from 'backward castes' including Mulayam Singh Yadav, and popular Dalit leaders, such as Kanshi Ram and Mayawati meant that Bachchan's nominal on-screen identification with the disenfranchised no longer carried the same resonance. Indeed, by 1991, Bachchan's on-screen persona of forced 'proletarianism' was almost entirely unsustainable.

Furthermore, as real-life violence in the country grew, with the terrorist attacks of the late 1980s, the Mandal Commission protests, and the assassination of Rajiv Gandhi, appetite for on-screen violence also declined. Through the early 1990s, on-screen violence became increasingly unpopular albeit more graphic, as real-life events threatened to overwhelm a nation that was desperate for economic growth and social security. It is significant that the Mumbai blasts, post-Ayodhya riots and the 'opening' of the Indian economy all occur in a short period of time from 1992 to 1993. The films of this period of upheaval reveal a propensity towards gore and the end of the 'angry young man' is embodied on screen by the 'psychotic hero', who marks a transition to different narratives (Mazumdar 2000: 238–64).[31]

At the same time, throughout the 1980s, there had been a steady – if imperceptible – economic growth in the country, a process that was phenomenally accelerated by the liberalisation policies announced in 1992. Unsurprisingly, with the privileging of steady social and economic growth, the 'aesthetic of mobilisation' that had unified a frustrated nation around Bachchan's star persona in the previous decades became untenable, if not outright dangerous in the 1990s. By 1994, and with the release of *Hum Aapke Hain Kaun* (What Am I to You, 1994), on-screen violence had run its course. This is not to suggest that action or violent films were no longer made, or that there weren't comedies and love stories to be found in the 1970s and 1980s, but that these were not the most successful films of their times.

Of course, Bachchan would rise again, with *KBC* and *Mohabbatein*, in 2000, but he would require a different star persona: the ageing patriarch offering both wise counsel and conservative validation for the country's neo-liberal aspirations. It is important to recognise that Bachchan's post-2000 persona does not entirely eschew the earlier strands, and the ageing policeman of *Khakee* (Uniform, 2004) and the godfather of *Sarkaar* (2005) owe much to his earlier screen persona. Similarly, films like *Cheeni Kum* (Less Sugar, 2007), and *Banti aur Babli* (Bunty and Babli, 2005) draw on the contradictions between Bachchan's off-screen power and sobriety and his on-screen willingness to embarrass himself for the audience's amusement.

One final aspect of Bachchan's stardom requires mention: Hindi cinema has traditionally offered few roles for ageing superstars. In the past, reigning stars either faded into 'character' roles, playing fathers to younger, more bankable stars: Dilip Kumar in *Shakti*, for example, plays Bachchan's father; or they moved behind the camera to take up production and direction: both Dev Anand and Raj Kapoor followed this route. In some cases, as with Anand, they attempted to extend their original star persona into old age, with diminishing returns, and eventual ridicule. There were few roles as protagonists for ageing stars, and indeed there are few meta-textual models for them; even in the epics, ageing warriors often serve as plot devices or obstacles against whom the protagonist can define himself. Although *Mohabbatein*, *Kabhi Khushi Kabhie Gham* and *Sarkar Raj* (2008) do cast Bachchan as the ageing patriarch for the younger hero to measure himself against, and challenge, other films continue to not only feature Bachchan as the protagonist, such as *Teen Patti* (Three Cards, 2010) and *Aarakshan* (Reservation, 2011) but also suggest ways in which new narratives can extend the actor's screen persona.

A corollary of this reinvention has been the range of filmmakers – both old and new – who realised they could work with Bachchan, draw on his earlier star persona, and capitalise

Echoes of *Zanjeer* in *Dev* (2004)

on his status commercially and critically, without having to resort to the 'attractions' that had circumscribed his performances at the height of his stardom. Younger directors created new narratives for the reinvented star image of rage, age, and visible vulnerability in films like *Black* and *Sarkar*, often expanding his earlier roles by incorporating the fragilities of age. Indeed the vengeful but grieving Subhash Nagre of *Sarkar* and *Sarkar Raj* or the loving husband of *Baghban* (Gardener, 2003) seem like older versions of the characters from *Don* or *Kasme Vade*. However, they are new iterations rather than parodies or copies and the reinvented star can now play 'even these hyper-masculine roles as men close to his own age, happily married patriarchs with grown children' (Chute 2005: unpaginated). In recent years, Bachchan has successfully straddled film and television, in roles that alternate between highlighting his growing physical fragility and evoking his erstwhile raging persona, many imbued with an increasingly urgent sense of both on-screen and off-screen mortality. The actor's first television series, *Yudh* (War, 2014) casts him as a powerful industrialist afflicted by a terminal illness while *Piku* (2015) features him as a frail, bowel-obsessed eccentric.

At the same time, the star's reinvention is a symptom of a novel development in cinema and popular culture as ageing heroes or patriarchs have had few roles in the cinema's long trajectory. In the epic texts, they serve as backdrop and generational opposition for younger heroes to defeat through symbolic or narrative patricide; in cinema, ageing stars are promoted to character roles that limit them to the *pater familias*, against whom younger stars can measure their on-screen power and off-screen influence. Moreover, patriarchal roles also tend to strip ageing stars of their sex appeal, constructing them entirely in paternal terms; even when accompanied by an on-screen spouse, the patriarch was appropriately and respectfully desexualised.

Bachchan's reinvented persona upturns this desexualised patriarch. In *K3G*, he cavorts with a bevy of scantily clad blondes until pulled up by his wife (played by his real-life spouse). The star reacts to his wife's chastisement by singing the opening lines of a popular cheeky, and overtly suggestive, number from *Ghulam* (Slave, 1998). The film also presents the two stars in a marriage that is both stable and long-lasting, which, despite complexities and frictions, remains affectionate and intimate. The failed gangster-caper *Boom* (2003) features the return of the 1970s sex siren, and Bachchan's frequent co-star, Zeenat Aman, as well as a guest appearance by the erstwhile American pin-up Bo Derek. The same year, Bachchan co-starred with Hema Malini, one of the

Baghban (2003)

biggest female stars of the 1970s in *Baghban*.[32] Although *Baghban* functions primarily as a family drama recapitulating popular themes of disruption and the eventual reconciliation of the joint family, the intensely emotional and intimate relationship between the two older stars indicates a shift in the ways of love: romance is no longer the sole preserve of the youthful, a point further driven home by the star duo in *Veer-Zaara* (2005). Even when shorn of a romantic partner, the star's sex appeal has been emphasised, despite or rather in addition to his status as the benevolent patriarch; *Kabhi Alvidaa Na Kehna* (Never Say Goodbye, 2005), for example, cast him as a wealthy widower whose wild sexual exploits leave his serious, married son bemused.

The fact that Bachchan can still command centre stage in his films suggests that his stardom may be entering another new phase that we cannot yet fully understand. Why and how does an ageing star maintain relevance, after nearly half a century, especially in a country where the overwhelming majority of the population is under forty? Gaffney and Holmes explain, 'Stars can restate, often in new and modern forms, old identities and values, as well as calling a society towards newer, and perhaps confused, emergent values and value systems'. (2007: 1). Bachchan's career allows us an extended period of time to examine these values and value systems: for example, we can see the outlines of social conservatism in films from the 1970s that in many ways open the path to the muscular Hindu nationalism of the 1990s.[33] While his privileged upbringing is in marked contrast to the obligatory ordinariness of his early roles, we can trace *KBC*'s suave host to those early screen appearances.[34] However, his more recent work is harder to analyse, especially without the benefit of hindsight or the necessary chronological distance. Yet, it is hard to imagine that, even now, Bachchan is not somehow heralding some newer or emergent values and value systems that which we at this moment can only intuit.

4 CREATION AND RE-CREATION OF A SUPER STAR

There is little doubt that cultural specificities inform the ways in which stars and stardom are constructed in India, the semiotic system(s) they invoke and embody, and the manner in which they are received by a culturally informed audience.[1] Indeed, Indian stars are constructed narratively, technically, and extra-textually in ways that are both similar to and different from Western film industries, including 'additional or alternate cultural paradigms and aesthetics' (Mishra *et al.* 1989: 51). As such, 'Bachchan is never simply the "star" or even "Vijay", but also *simultaneously* the "industrial hero", a figure imbued with epic/mythic meanings (the "illegitimate" Karna), the powerful mobilizer of the urban underclass, among many other things' (Sen 2013: 8). This chapter considers the alternative cultural paradigms that are evoked by Bachchan's star text and imbue it with epic and mythical meanings. These epic/mythic significances appear to be neither accidental nor unconscious, as multiple films locate their narratives and characters in dominant meta-texts, thus making it necessary to examine their contribution to the construction of stars, especially one as dominant and enduring as Bachchan.

Understanding how different cultural paradigms contribute to Bachchan's stardom necessitates a consideration not only of meta-texts but also culturally specific narrative devices, and aesthetic and philosophical concepts. This requires building on earlier analyses of the star in the context of the mythical figures of *Karna* and *Arjuna*, and extending those to examine the reinvention of his screen persona as a patriarchal figure in films such as *Mohabbatein*, *Kabhi Khushi Kabhie Gham*, *Baghban*, and *Khakee*, as evocative of *Bhishma* and *Daśaratha*.

Culturally specific aspects of spectatorship that inform the consumption of film narratives and star images are also briefly discussed, including the practice of *darśana*[2] as a unique aspect of performance, its recognition and acceptance by the culturally knowledgeable viewer, and the location of the narratives – and the star embodying these – in the aesthetic and philosophical context of *rasa*. Examination of these is necessary given their continued significance in viewing practices as well as narrative structures, conventions of performance, and technical choices such the use of frontality and direct address.[3]

Star as the mythical hero

A star may be defined as a 'performer in a particular medium whose figure enters into subsidiary forms of circulation, and then feeds back into future performances' (Ellis 1992: 19). A star's image is thus created over several films, transcends individual roles, performances and film texts, and any performance of the star image of a character in a particular film must also engage and negotiate with the star's overall persona. Unsurprisingly, across a number of films, a star's image is maintained and reinforced by specific types of roles, costumes, and presentations and many stars prefer to stick to similar roles as a means of satisfying 'audience expectations'.[4] The post-independence success of the star triumvirate of Raj Kapoor, Dilip Kumar, and Dev Anand, with clear delineation of roles, narratives and parallel texts inscribed this as popular industry 'wisdom', with few stars venturing too far from their established screen personas. There is also an impetus to capitalise on a successful star persona by other stakeholders, including directors and producers, which often makes any avoidance of typecasting difficult. In Bachchan's case, as the budgets for his films skyrocketed – and within a short span of time, from the success of *Zanjeer* to that of *Sholay* – the benefits of maintaining a star image became not only obvious but also necessary not only for the actor, but for many in the industry around him.

Beyond the profit motive, in India, like other major industries, a 'star text is created within the films themselves as vehicles for star performances which in turn build on images in other films and in other media to give them roles as national icons of beauty, desire and utopian beings' (Dwyer 2000: 118–19). Stardom also draws on extra-filmic information, and from multiple media, including drama, literature, and art, to locate the performer within a particular cultural context and dominant texts and archetypes become reference points that a star text may echo, reference, emulate, challenge, and/or subvert. This location of a particular film and character in a star's oeuvre and its relationship with wider culture is part of the spectatorial pleasure offered by a successful star text that can combine on-screen persona, the real life of the actor, and the zeitgeist, while also transcending immediate temporality to reference larger cultural themes, symbols, and concerns. Perhaps one way of understanding Bachchan's unparalleled stardom is to consider not only the ways in which his on-screen image serves as an expression of the national zeitgeist and a symbolic articulation of national aspirations, but also as a series of intersections of a parallel text that conflates his star persona with much-loved, well-known and influential Hindu epic narratives.

Furthermore, 'as complex signs embodying historical, cultural and economic meanings, Bombay stars are cultural "compromises" of a bewildering complexity' (Mishra 2002: 126) and any reading must also admit the possibility of a range of other, potentially conflicting readings. It is thus imperative to recognise that the star's narrative occupies the interstice of myth and national icon of desire, in addition to embodying multiple sites of contested identities in modern India – of language, region, caste, class, and religion – and cannot fully be understood without this larger meta-textual context. In Bachchan's case, this provides a particularly rich seam as his films span multiple decades and political transformations, and his star text draws upon multiple aspects of India's key epics, the *Mahābhārata* and the *Rāmāyana*, to remain relevant and popular.[5]

Bachchan's star text is initially based on the heroes of the *Mahābhārata* with his on-screen rebellion coded in mythic terms as his 'film persona challenged the figure of the noble, transcendent Rāma as the *dhārmik* model of the hero', relying instead on the 'features that belonged to the antihero Karna in the *Mahābhārata* …' (ibid: 128). The *Mahābhārata*'s heroes form the basis of the star's early persona, driven as they are by righteous anger and, in different ways, and inhabiting the margins of a society riven by conflict and despair. Moreover, the only narrative option available to these mythical heroes, as for Bachchan's angry young man, is victory against all odds or a glorious death. This meta-textual link is forged and emphasised in films including *Zanjeer*, *Deewar*, *Sholay*, and *Muqaddar ka Sikandar*.

The *Mahābhārata* seems the most appropriate meta-text for a particularly tumultuous socio-political period and its themes and personas found their way into popular cinema, culminating eventually in overt references, even in film titles – and not only for Bachchan's films – such as *Aaj ka Arjun* (Today's Arjuna, 1990) and *Chakravyuha* (The Labyrinth, 1983). Bachchan's parallel text, during this period, moreover, deployed and conflated these themes in multiple subtle and intricate ways.

An explicit link with the *Mahābhārata* epic is forged early on with *Zanjeer* and an initial articulation of the Arjuna persona, of a warrior taking up arms against a more powerful enemy.

In the *Mahābhārata*, Arjuna is the greatest of warriors, and his quest – along with his brothers, the five Pandavas – is framed as a righteous one, with justice as its goal, although rivalry with his cousins, the Kauravas, and finally revenge are also motivations. While elements of Arjuna's persona, including his amatory success, exuberance, and social and artistic skills would only be woven fully into Bachchan's star text after 1977, the film's evocation of *Mahābhārata*'s *dharmik* hero is explicit: *Zanjeer*'s Vijay also breaks the law, or at least goes against the letter of it, and his victory at the end of the film provides retroactive justification for all his transgressions. Like Arjuna, Vijay too questions the morality of his illegal actions and consciously determines that transgressions are not only acceptable, but also righteous. The narrative impulse of *Zanjeer*, as with later films drawing on this archetype, including *Trishul*, *Kaala Patthar*, and P*arvarish* (Upbringing, 1977), ensures the protagonist's victory. While he may face great odds, and even pay a price – often in the guise of the death of a close friend – there is no other narrative option for Arjuna.[6] Favoured by gods and men, and endowed with myriad physical, emotional, and material attractions, Arjuna is the archetypal hero, predestined to win. Although Arjuna is a powerful, resonant, mythical force, he is perhaps too much of a victor, especially for the 1970s to adequately reflect the nation's anxieties and despair. Unsurprisingly, Bachchan's screen persona became far more closely intertwined with that of Karna soon after *Zanjeer*. Perhaps it is inevitable, as the two heroes stand as counterpoints and mirror images in the epic, and the traumatic changes of the era could only be embodied in a hero who loses comprehensively at every juncture of his narrative: Karna.

As Kunti's illegitimate eldest son, Karna stands in complete contrast to Arjuna: abandoned at birth, he grows up to be a great warrior, but is consistently denied his birthright as a warrior of royal blood. He is often mocked, insulted, and humiliated by the Pandavas, who are, by blood at least, his brothers. Instead, his talent is recognised by Duryodhana, the leader of the Kauravas, who brings him into his court, and honours him as a warrior.[7] Karna's loyalty to the Kauravas, despite his personal reservations, ensures that he enters the war on the 'wrong' side, doomed not by a lack of morality but by an excess of it.

Deewar is the most overt retelling of Karna's story in recent years.[8] The film effectively draws links between Karna and 1970s cinema's 'urban warrior', as exemplified by Bachchan's Vijay, emphasising his marginality, denial of heritage, and the despair that fills his life until a tragic, and violent, death.[9] Karna is a potent symbol for the newly urban masses who could find a 'sense of pride and performance, without losing the experience of a deep anguish' in the narrative of 'a powerful force whose individual and aggressive posturing could give voice to the wretched, discarded and marginalised outsiders' (Mazumdar 2007: 12). Perhaps the anxieties of dislocation and dispossession brought about by rapid industrialisation and urbanisation could only be reflected by Karna, the only hero in the Indic tradition to be dispossessed not only narratively but also in the country's cosmo-geography: there are no major mythical landmarks linked to Karna, and he has little religious or mythical presence in the country's temples and ritual spaces.[10]

Furthermore, *Deewar*, 'is not the eternal play of the epic, but a historical reworking of its ethical and philosophical dimension' (ibid: 14). It locates the anxieties of dispossession and defeat at the heart of the country's industrial and urban centre, modernising both the hero and his narrative.[11] It is this historical reworking of Karna's ethical confrontation with foes overtly identified as 'moral' that enabled *Deewar* to capture the country's zeitgeist: Vijay the 'elder' and Karna-like figure critiques the hollow morality of the 'system', and is punished for it, with death by his brother's hand, an act that has been sanctioned by his mother.[12] Ravi, the policeman, is presented as righteous as he repeats clichés about principles and upholds a law that is brutal and dehumanising; yet his actions, including killing Vijay, are rewarded not only by material signs of approval – the film is framed in a ceremony by the police department to honour Ravi's bravery – but also the mother's undivided and unchallenged affection.[13]

In the epic, Karna's death is caused in great part by his mother, Kunti, depriving him of his magical armour that renders him invincible and is his sole physical inheritance from his father. The loss of his armour leaves Karna unprotected and excises the sole physical link to his birth identity. In *Deewar*, Vijay's talismanic badge evokes Karna's armour, and its loss in the final chase sequence seals his fate. Like Karna, who is killed in contravention of the martial code when he is helpless and unarmed, Vijay too is killed when he is at his most vulnerable. And Vijay, like Karna, knows and accepts that his mother has chosen her law-abiding/legitimate son over him.[14]

With *Deewar*, Bachchan's on-screen persona as Karna, righteous albeit not legal, and doomed to failure and death by circumstances, and his choices, is established for the first time. It is a persona that films like *Sholay* and *Muqaddar ka Sikandar* develop further. Yet the star's persona is not of Karna alone, perhaps because total defeat also engenders a total lack of hope, and that is unsustainable for any star text over an extended period of time. Moreover, with the imposition of the Emergency, and a resurgence of socio-political conservatism, it was inevitable that Karna's lone, dispossessed rebellion would be defeated by Arjuna's establishmentarian stance.

As such, a parallel strand of films continues the Arjuna narrative, providing hope, and conformity, in films like *Parvarish*, *Suhaag* (Matrimony, 1979), *Amar Akbar Anthony*, and *Naseeb*. In these, Bachchan plays the caring hero who protects the weak, the obedient younger brother (*Amar Akbar Anthony*) following the elder brother's lead, the caring son who not only forgives but also continues to love an errant father figure (*Suhaag* and *Naseeb*) thereby echoing Arjuna's love for Bhishma and Dronācarya. These films also explore other aspects of Arjuna's narrative, offering romance and comedy, both elements of the epic text.[15] Moreover, the overt resonances of Karna initiated by *Deewar* are also unsustainable over time and through multiple films because their unrelenting grimness and the inevitability of a tragic end make any evolution or extension of the character or narrative impossible. Unsurprisingly, even films like *Sholay* and *Muqaddar ka Sikandar*, which reference Karna's dispossession, also leaven the narrative and the star's performance with glimmers of hope, by easing the hero's isolation. Inevitably, not only does the mood lighten in later films, extending Bachchan's repertoire with comedy and romance, but the narratives employ more particular aspects of Arjuna, including cross-dressing, gender-bending, and disguise.

While an element of homoeroticism had informed Bachchan's star persona beginning with *Zanjeer*, a natural corollary of the construction of his hyper-masculine image,[16] a move away from the anguished Karna to that of the aesthete-warrior Arjuna opens up multiple possibilities that inform – and subvert – his angry young man persona, queering it not only at the point of reception but at the moment of image production.[17]

Bachchan's on-screen hyper- masculinity was insistently contradicted by his introverted, sensitive, off-screen narrative and was undermined onscreen by his early 'middle-class' roles. However, after *Deewar*, his roles are subverted, at times by the inclusion of comic elements that spoof masculine strength as in *Amar Akbar Anthony*, or by maudlin sentimentality as in *Sharaabi*, or by intense homosocial bonds and narratives in films like *Sholay* and *Dostana*. The inherent instability of his hyper-masculine construct reaches its obvious culmination with Bachchan's overt transvestism in *Lawaaris*, with the song 'Mere Angne Mein'.[18]

These cultural constructions of simultaneously asserted and subverted masculinities, queered at the point of production, expand the character – and by extension, the star's – sexual appeal, and are closely aligned with *Mahābhārata*'s Arjuna, who repeatedly dresses in female clothing, and acts out female parts, without ever relinquishing his status as the martial hero.[19] Indeed, given the multiple ways Bachchan's on-screen appearances and off-screen persona queer his star text, a closer study is warranted into not only constructions of masculinity in the actor's oeuvre but also of representations of gender and sexuality in Hindi cinema as a whole.[20]

End of the angry young man

However, by the mid-1980s, even the multifaceted Arjuna was not enough to sustain Bachchan's star persona. By the end of the decade, the actor had finally reached the end of the righteous warrior parallel text: post-Bofors, the audience had decided that this was no Arjuna/Karna attempting to uphold *dharma*. Instead Bachchan seemed increasingly weary onscreen and beleaguered offscreen by political and financial troubles. Somewhere, Arjuna and Karna had been replaced by an ageing Bhishma, caught in the dogma of *dharma* rather than its actual practice.

At the same time, changing social, political, and economic circumstances meant that, by the early 1990s, the nation required other narratives to embody and express its hopes. Inevitably, like in the *Mahābhārata*, the levels of violence in the country had increased steadily from 1984 to 1992, acquiring horrific, near mythic proportions, and crossing over into *adharma* and injustice. The demolition of the Babri Masjid followed by the Bombay riots marked a watershed in the popular imaginary: sectarian violence would not disappear in India after this date, but there would be a growing sense of weariness with the frequency and increasing ferocity of the outbursts.

By 1994, the nation seemed to have exhausted its thirst for violence, righteous or otherwise. The action films of the late 1980s also indicated a growing shift towards gore as contrasted with earlier, restrained on-screen violence. These were also a corollary of shifting film-viewing patterns: the proliferation of televisions and videocassettes, along with increased film piracy, through the 1980s meant that families, especially women, limited their trips to film theatres. In turn, theatres turned their attention to young, mostly proletarian men, who were enticed by films deemed 'unsuitable' for 'family consumption': gore and sexually graphic material became crucial to theatre owners desperate to attract audiences.[21]

For Bachchan, *Agneepath* (Path of Fire, 1990)[22] marks the culmination of his earlier star text, with its mythic resonances of Karna and Arjuna. The film requires consideration especially as it attempts to recreate the earlier Vijay and loosely replicates – or more accurately – parodies *Deewar*. Now considered a 'cult hit', the film retains the basic outlines of the earlier text: a father, wrongly humiliated and killed, a family exiled from the 'idyllic' village to the big city, the initial travails of the child, again named Vijay, who must not only survive but also protect his widowed mother and young sibling. However, unlike *Deewar*'s epic fratricidal conflict, *Agneepath* introduces a loyal, comic sidekick who can support the hero in his fights. It is this sidekick, Krishnan (Mithun Chakravarty), who marries Vijay's sister and is adopted by his mother as the 'good son'.

Unlike *Deewar*, the enemy here is not the general brutalising 'system' but is personalised in a criminal named Kancha Cheena (Danny Denzongpa) who engineers the father's humiliation and murder. The film perfunctorily references the iconic scene of *Deewar*'s Vijay polishing shoes on the city streets, although he is no longer the innocent child steadily brutalised by urban poverty. *Agneepath*'s Vijay, even as a child is already the hardened, street smart, tough guy, ready to bend or break the law as necessary.

This Vijay does not attempt honest work at the docks before being lured into crime; instead arming himself with a knife, he obsessively follows Kancha. Unlike *Deewar*'s Vijay, who throws a stone in his childish, impotent anger, this child's rage finds immediate relief in burning down one of Kancha's petrol stations. If *Deewar* had offered a 'pleasurable subversion without undermining the supremacy of the law' (Prasad 1998: 152), the law in *Agneepath*, despite the nominal presence of the upstanding but ineffective Commissioner Gaitonde (Vikram Gokhale) is almost entirely absent.

Elements of *Deewar* are replicated, though with little psychological coherence or emotional impact: Vijay's memories of his father's murder proffer no explanation for his actions. He marries and has a child, although the feisty Anita is replaced now by the servile Mary (Madhavi). In contrast to the romance between Vijay and Anita which was modern and relatively egalitarian, in *Agneepath*, the courtship is non-existent and the eventual relationship is abusive and threatening, with little by way of explicit consent from Mary. The marginalisation of female characters that had accompanied the rise of the superstar reaches a nadir and Mary's only role is to serve Vijay's needs and listen to his rants. A similar fate awaits the other women in the film: the sister Shiksha (Neelam) serves as eye candy and a perfunctory plot point. The mother too does no more than occasionally, if mildly, berate Vijay for abandoning his father's principles. Although the final death scene echoes the one from *Deewar*, with Vijay dying in his mother's lap, the focus remains wholly on the superstar.

The film perfunctorily strings together multiple 'clap worthy' attractions from other Bachchan films but is plagued by poor production values and a lack of attention to filmic techniques. *Agneepath* attempts to recreate the post-*Coolie* attraction of the star's miraculous on-screen recovery by including a rush to the hospital, an emergency surgery, and recovery.

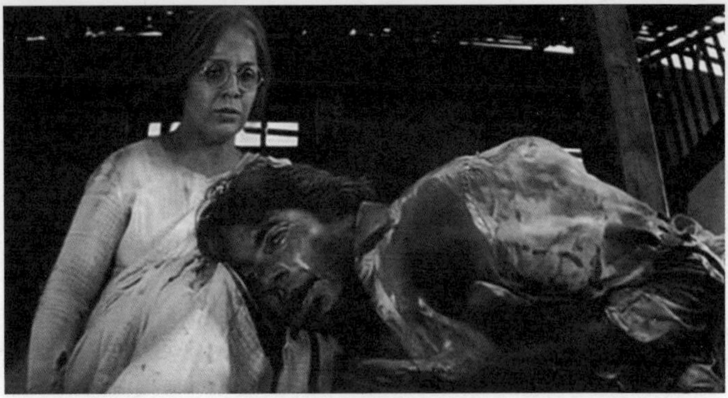

End of the 'angry young man.' *Agneepath* (1990)

It even nods to the iconic balcony scene from *Coolie*, with the actor thanking his supporters at the entrance of the hospital. However, in *Agneepath*, the mob clamouring and rioting outside the hospital is made up entirely of Vijay's thugs.

Agneepath's Vijay remains an achronism with expensive white suits and designer shoes signalling the wealthy superstar even as he rants about the needs of the poor. In a particularly incoherent sequence, he storms at the patrons of an expensive restaurant for disrespecting him. His fury is apparently triggered by the reaction of the patrons, yet the murmured voices seem more admiring than contemptuous, thus complicating Vijay's reaction: why does the acceptance of the elite matter to him? Is this approval entirely withheld or is his reaction – at least – partially based in paranoia? Moreover, his anger is not directed at the elite patrons of the restaurants but focused on the terrified waiter. This then is no John Jani Janardhan of *Naseeb* or Iqbal of *Coolie*, who understands and identifies with the urban proletariat. This isn't even Vijay of *Deewar* whose manners impeccably aligned him with the elite even as his loyalty to his fellow dockworkers endeared him to the poor.

Moreover, the film's conclusion is also very different from *Deewar*, which depicts the re-establishment of a social and moral order, albeit a conservative one. Vijay may be dead, but his family is rewarded and honoured for their sacrifice. The film ends then on a similar note to most popular retellings of the *Mahābhārata*, at the juncture when the war is won, and a 'righteous' kingdom restored. *Agneepath* culminates in a grimmer, more dystopic vision from the epic that is often overlooked in the popular imagination. In this reiteration, Vijay's death may happen in his 'home' and on his mother's lap but the survivors are left with nothing but an apocalyptic landscape. The final scenes of the film are reminders of a less-loved and -known section of the epic where grieving women from both sides join to mourn their dead amidst the vast destruction wrought by the war. In this bleak version of the tale, neither heroes nor morality can or indeed may survive.[23]

Agneepath and its apocalyptic finale signal an absolute end to the narrative of the angry young man with echoes of Karna and Arjuna. Jain makes a persuasive link between the 'aggressive Ram of the Ayodhya campaign', noting that 'neither have been possible, *nor necessary*, without the lean, active, hungry, fighting, and labouring, libidinalized screen presence' and 'his resolutely non abject embodiment of the urban working-class male from the early 1970s through the 1980s' (2007: 340). It may also be argued that the demolition of the Babri mosque and the 1992 Mumbai riots are also when the country reaches satiation with on-screen violence and begins to seek an aesthetic and narrative of stability. Indeed *Agneepath*'s apocalyptic on-screen narrative, all too close to the violence convulsing the nation, also marks the culmination of the *Mahābhārata*, and a warning to seek narratives beyond the battlefield.

Agneepath's psychological incoherence also marks the beginning of the short and brutal period of the 'psychotic hero' played by Shah Rukh Khan in three back-to-back films: *Darr* (Fear, 1993), *Baazigar* (Player, 1993), and the aptly named, *Anjaam* (Conclusion, 1994). The psychotic hero 'seems to question the more "rational", restrained and controlled anger of the Bachchan era', which portrayed a 'wronged man, unstable but always "morally bound", an outlaw but committed to the family…' (Mazumdar 2000: 252). One could argue that the period between *Agneepath* in 1990 and *Anjaam* in 1994 is the most politically unstable and brutally violent in the history of post-independence India. Perhaps then, 'the psychotic image seeks to generate a new discourse of pain, dispersed morality, and a violent drive towards death – a response to our own catastrophe' (ibid: 251). If *Agneepath* marks the end of any kind of 'rational' and 'restrained' violence, symbolically signalled by a final apocalyptic destruction, the film also opens the narrative possibilities for the 'psychotic hero', who can reflect, express, and symbolically process the pain the nation seems intent on repeatedly inflicting on itself. However, it may be argued that the 'psychotic hero' has little long term narrative future, except to imitate or perhaps even parody an earlier apocalypse, and thus serves only as a bridge to another archetype.

Indeed this period, with the concurrent strands of Bachchan's decline and Khan's rise to stardom, also marks the transition between two meta-texts, with narratives moving from the *Mahābhārata*'s battlefields to dreams of *Rāmarājya*, the peaceful and prosperous kingdom established by Rāma on his return from exile in the *Rāmayana*. These two images are crucial to the Indian imaginary, symbolically conceptualising human life as a cosmic struggle in the first instance, and as prosperous status quo in the second. Indeed, the star texts of the two biggest stars of the industry not only provide a fascinating glimpse of the zeitgeist of the times of each, but also indicate the ways in which India's two epic master texts resonate, reflect and make sense of contemporary reality.

If Bachchan's star text was rooted in the 'imaginary fulfilment of the slum dweller's own fantasies' (Mishra 2002: 128), Khan's star persona is rooted in the rise of the post-liberalisation middle class, and may even be linked to the rise of Hindu nationalism with its focus on Rāma as the locus of national imagination. This renewal of *Rāmāyana* as a central subtext of Hindi cinema is often located in the 'new middle-class culture of Hindu nationalism, which is currently engaged in reinterpreting Indian history to silence Muslims, denying the simultaneity of such multiple traditions' (Dwyer 2000: 16). There is, of course, little evidence of a 'direct, unmediated, connection between the popular and Hindutva politics' (Mishra 2002: 233).

Moreover, many such readings, focusing on the rise of Hindu nationalism, ignore other aspects of the 1990s, which was characterised also by economic liberalisation, remarkable economic growth, and the coming of age of a completely post-nationalist polity which referenced not past achievements but rather future aspirations.[24] The period beginning in 1992 was also marked by unprecedented contact for most Indians with the world, as satellite television, music channels, and foreign consumer brands entered the country. Thc film industry also experienced a renaissance as new technologies and narratives enticed audiences back into movie theatres and the export market for Hindi cinema grew exponentially. As such, the transition between the two epics, as marked by star texts of Bachchan and Khan, provides interesting insights into evolving stardom, national narratives, and zeitgeists.[25]

The enduring age of the patriarch

By the mid-1990s, Bachchan seemed finished as a film star. Tired recapitulations of his earlier on-screen persona in films like *Mrityudaata* (Executioner, 1997), *Major Saab* (The Major, 1998), *Lal Badshaah* (Red King, 1999), and *Suryavansham* (Lineage of the Sun, 1999) were commercial and critical failures. Even *Bade Miyan, Chhote Miyan* (Big Guy, Little Guy, 1998),

The years of wilderness. With Soundarya in *Sooryavansham* (1999)

which tried to capitalise on Bachchan's impeccable comic timing posted only moderate commercial success, which many attributed to his younger co-star, Govinda. These films seemed unable to use the star in any effective manner, merely stringing together a series of 'attractions' associated with his earlier roles. As such, an 'item' song, a fight sequence, a perfunctory romance, a few aggressive dialogues, and some variation of a comic scene seemed all that any script could imagine for Bachchan.

This losing streak finally ended with *Mohabbatein*, a film that brought together a flailing Bachchan and Shah Rukh Khan, the new superstar, the first on-screen point of contact between the two star texts, that also offered Bachchan a plausible way forward in an era that appeared to privilege stability over revolution, negotiation over fighting, and brains and charm over brawn.

In the film, Bachchan played the autocratic, patrician, school principal that Khan, playing Raj Aryan, a young music teacher, must face and defeat. Bachchan's persona was successfully recast as that of the ascetic disciplinarian, Bhishma[26] from the *Mahābhārata*. In the epic, Bhishma[27] is the life-long celibate warrior, father figure to both branches of the family, the reluctant leader of the Kaurava army, and, on his death bed, the advisor and teacher to Yudhishthir, the eldest of the Pandavas. In many ways, Bhishma's persona is the symbolic culmination of Arjuna's innate conservatism and Karna's blind loyalty, as both end in a rigid and petrified adherence to rules that are removed from social needs and human warmth.

Bachchan's Narayan Shankar was brilliant casting, especially in contrast to Khan's Raj Aryan as an idealised, fraternal figure whose only interest is the happiness of his young students. By setting up Shankar as the grim immovable obstacle to Raj's exuberant warmth, the film cleverly deploys the star personas of both actors: the not-so-young angry man is challenged not by an opponent who is angrier or stronger, but one who refuses to fight.

The film's backstory has Raj falling in love with Megha (Aishwarya Rai), Shankar's daughter. Referencing earlier tragic love stories, Raj is 'exiled' and Megha commits suicide. However, in a twist to the convention of tragic love, and even revenge stories, Raj's incognito return to the school is not to bring about Shankar's downfall but to share the love he still feels for Megha with the lonely, bitter man who has renounced all human contact. The film's structure allows an overlap between the personas and symbols of the two epic texts, clearly evoking the early portions of *Rāmāyana* where merely the sight of a young Ram is enough to melt the hardest of hearts.[28]

The film also almost entirely eschews romance for its two leading stars: Narayan Shankar is celibacy personified while Raj's love interest is dead. Instead, the film is almost completely framed as a contest between models of masculinities.[29] Raj's entrance on screen is mythically coded, prolonged by the camera peering over his shoulder as he is preceded, literally, by flowers and smiles. Moreover, Raj's ability to establish more humane rules and overturn earlier customs endows this particular cinematic role with immense resonance. In one of the subplots of the film, he encourages a student to woo a young widow, indicating that even age-old customs may be overturned for human purposes. In contrast, Shankar is framed as a man trapped by a hollow value system, whose adherence to the letter of the law rather than the human spirit has even led to his daughter's death. Although *Mohabbatein* reiterates the conflict between the letter of the law and its spirit that the angry young man had experienced in the 1970s, it also suggests a particularly neo-liberal solution, that the individual quest for humanity and kindness be the preferred method for effecting change.

More importantly, the film refuses to allow Bachchan any of his familiar 'attractions'. He has no songs; indeed he shows up repeatedly at the ends of songs to throw a damper on festivities. There are no fight sequences and Shankar does not countenance laughter. However, by restraining the star physically, the film emphasises his fading physical strength and growing vulnerability while evoking both the rage and power of days past.

The climax of the film brings together the two stars in an antagonistic encounter that signals the shift that has occurred in audience identifications and preferences. Shankar remains isolated and enraged, recalling Bachchan's earlier screen persona, except the righteous anger has now decayed to bitterness and narcissism. Instead, Raj is positioned as the hero although his victory lies not in vanquishing the enemy but in winning him over.

The film's conclusion offers the spectator an emotionally rich and extra-textually layered pleasure: the rage is quenched while the epic warrior Bhishma is portrayed with the equanimity that he had legendarily maintained on his death bed. The patriarch's acceptance of his own frailty and willingness to learn new rules extends an affirmation to a country in the midst of enormous cultural change that the 'new' values need not negate the old. Finally, for an audience brought up on the enacted, recited and retold *Rāmāyana*, the film's conclusion delivers a rare pleasure, one that the literary text of *Rāmāyana* or its more

Bachchan reinvented as the patriarch of the nation on TV with *Kaun Banega Crorepati*

traditional retellings cannot provide: the spectacle of a grieving Daśaratha expressing his remorse for sending Rāma into exile.

That same year Bachchan also debuted on television as the host of *KBC*. If *Mohabbatein* had softened the superstar's brooding persona, *KBC* not only re-established the star as a significantly marketable commodity on screen – both large and small – but also facilitated 'the reinvention of a celluloid icon into a transmedia star' (Mitra 2012: 568). In many ways, the disciplinarian headmaster of *Mohabbatein* and *KBC*'s quiz master were linked, and reinforced each other, especially in their focus on knowledge (Mishra 2002: 154). However, unlike the earlier era where proficiencies were valued for their own sake or for principles, education was now explicitly linked with material success. With Bachchan at the forefront of this new era of information as a route to wealth, consumerist aspirations were not only validated, but also imbued with an urbane glamour that laid to rest any arriviste worries.[30]

At the same time, by harnessing television's 'primary aesthetic properties – immediacy, intimacy and spontaneity' (Murray 2005) the quiz show format presented Bachchan as 'himself', or rather a version of himself that allowed seemingly 'real' interactions with the studio audience and contestants while simultaneously drawing on his larger-than-life screen persona: 'Though Amitabh Bachchan's cultural cache (sic) as the nation's erstwhile superstar was crucial to the dissemination and circulation of his star text' television as a medium could effectively deconstruct and demythologise the star to ensure his 'reinvention as the familiar, genial and effusive paternal figure' (Mitra 2012: 574).

KBC's contribution to this reinvention cannot be over emphasised. The star's unusually tall and lanky physique, controlled body language and memorable baritone voice in the early 1970s had combined to create his unique star persona.[31] Indeed, 'Bachchan's is a goal-driven, instrumentalized body, its noisy (*dhishoom-dhishoom*) power derived from its own immanent hunger' (Jain 2007: 344). Bachchan's often seemingly outsized limbs were actively employed in fight sequences, song-and-dance sequences, and often slapstick comic routines with energy and enthusiasm. Moreover, as the star grew through the 1970s and 1980s, to tower in real life over his rivals, and onscreen over his enemies, technical conventions enhanced his grandeur and distance from the masses: 'The commonest shot used to photograph him is a full frontal, medium close-up or low-angle shot, in which he appears indubitably monumental' (Bhattacharya 2013: 155).

Television, as a medium, of course has no use for Bachchan's big-screen physicality and although he had not been considered 'a star of the facial close-up' (Jain 2007: 344), *KBC* primarily involved medium shots and close-ups of his upper body and face. Instead of the god-like distance from the masses he had claimed to save on the big screen, television now humbled and humanised the actor, bringing him to the eye level of not only the contestant seated before him but of the non-studio audiences watching at home. Moreover, without a script that at least nominally gave the illusion of playing a fictional role, the success of the show rested almost entirely on Bachchan's ability to deploy his on-screen persona while also convincing the audience of the 'authenticity' required by the medium.

Mohabbatein's technique of limiting the star's on-screen physicality to minimal movement also translated well on the small screen. *KBC*'s camera restricted the star body to a chair, primarily through a series of medium shots that focused on Bachchan's mostly still upper body.[32] Even as he delivered lines from some of his most famous films, the small screen constrained his physicality by requiring him to still his energetic, often wayward limbs. For the ageing star, perhaps accustomed to a default use of his limbs on camera, the change was dramatic: in restraining his body for the small screen, Bachchan gained both stillness and gravitas. The small screen thus 'magnified the Bachchan-phenomenon', opening up possibilities for a star persona that relied more on a restrained physicality and a studied stillness which, in his big-screen appearances, would be imbued with severity and grandeur, reinforcing his earlier superstar status while also allowing him a new lease of on-screen life.

This combination of tightly leashed physical expression and monumental stature was effectively used in the 2001 opulent family saga *Kabhi Khushi Kabhie Gham* (hereafter K3G). The film again pitted Bachchan against Khan as two generations of an affluent family. In an explicit re-articulation of the *Rāmāyana*, the film cast the industry's latest heart-throb, Hrithik Roshan, as the devoted younger brother. The film's pleasure is located in the detailed articulation of some of the emotional aspects of *Rāmāyana*: the sorrow of an exiled Rāma, the lack of maternal guidance that worries his wife who follows him into exile, his younger brother's loneliness, his mother's grief, and the misguided pride that masks his father's pain. The film ends with the return of the exiled son into the family fold, with the fulsome emotions of the reconciliation offering the spectatorial pleasures denied by the epic text.

The film sealed Bachchan's reinvention as the patriarchal figure who, despite being initially lost and embittered or proud, could both experience and extend benevolence and affection. A key part of this renewed image was an explicit acknowledgement of the star's physical frailty and emotional wounds. Indeed, the new persona held a moral authority, a righteous outrage (rather than rage), 'which is the grown up distillation of his youthful anger' (Chute 2005). This aspect of Bachchan's stardom warrants further study, in part because it challenges earlier narratives of ageing patriarchs who would make way for the new generation, not only in public but also in private spheres. If indeed,

> roles must not subvert the linearity of the four stages of man's life articulated in Hindu philosophy (*brahmacarya*, the student stage, *grhastha*, the stage of the family man, *vanaprastha*, retreat to the forest, and *sanyasa*, final renunciation of the world) and must conform to the ultimate Law (i.e., Dharma) (Mishra et al. 1989: 52).

Bachchan's post-2000 star persona entirely upsets this maxim. This is even more intriguing, given India's predominantly youthful population that stands in contrast to its greying political, social, and economic elite.[33]

Before concluding, a particular mention must be made of *Satyagraha* (Force of Truth, 2013), directed by the veteran 'parallel cinema' director, Prakash Jha, that places Bachchan in a Gandhian mode.[34] Despite only moderate commercial success, the film suggests interesting insights well as perhaps a prescient view into the future of Bachchan's star text and stardom.

The star plays an idealistic, retired teacher, Dwarka Anand, who loses his son Akhilesh (Indraneil Sengupta) to the

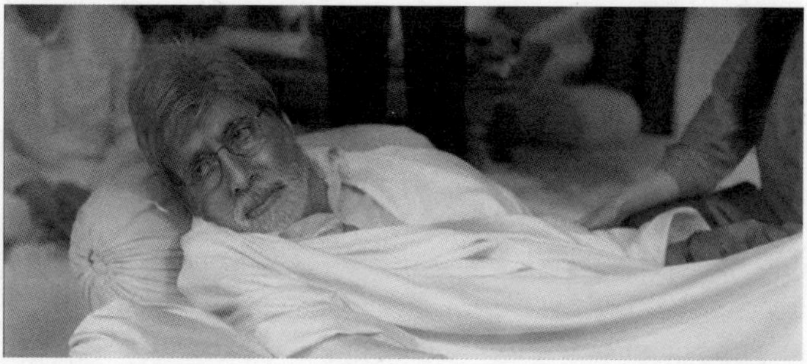

Satyagraha (2013)

machinations of corrupt police, bureaucracy, and politicians, but then inspires a motley group of young activists to political action.[35]

The film recreates sequences that are evocative of the state's crackdown on not only the anti-corruption protests but also the use of teargas and water-cannons during protests against the Delhi gang-rape of December 2012.[36] Drawing on the anti-corruption protest that erupted in India in 2011, the film traces Dwarka's increasing urgency and frustration that takes him from slapping a bureaucrat to his Gandhi-like fast-unto-death. An updated version of Gandhi's favourite *bhajan*, *Raghupati Raghav Raja Ram*, forms the title song and emphasises both the narrative continuity with India's history as well as the rupture from it. The song's lyrics do not raise a prayer for understanding and empathy as in the original *bhajan*, but demand less tolerance in the face of injustice. The film also creates sequences that evoke the nationalist struggle under Gandhi: Dwarka is shown not only fasting in public but also in poses familiar from newsreels and photographs of the national hero, including a shot when he leans heavily on his daughter-in-law and Yasmin (Kareena Kapoor) for support. Iconic props including Dwarka's wire-framed, roundish spectacles and white shawl are also employed to invoke familiar images of Gandhi, as is Dwarka's despairing plea 'Hey Ram'.

Dwarka's death, by a bullet, fired by a henchman of the corrupt politicians, recalls not only Gandhi's martyrdom, but also the star's earlier films, including *Deewar*, *Sholay*, and *Agneepath*, but with a key difference: Dwarka dies on camera and surrounded by his adoring acolytes, and his death is broadcast live and recorded for posterity. With the film's 'live broadcast' of the death scene, Bachchan's stardom and off-screen materiality collapse into a single narrative of an incessant public spectacle for the nation, a point that is driven home by the film's credits that pan over a candle-lit memorial of the grieving masses, dominated by a large, garlanded photograph of the star.

However, beyond immediate zeitgeist, the sequence also unites two significant moments from the two epics: Bhishma's sermon on his death-bed in *Mahābhārata* and Daśaratha's demise from grief on being parted from his son in the *Rāmāyana*. The rich polysemy of the sequence – political, historical, and with simultaneous resonances from both epics – proffers a glimpse into Bachchan's cross-generational appeal as well as indicating possible new narratives for the star-patriarch.

As seen above, Bachchan's star text is informed by and resonates with a rich polysemy, drawing not only on India's socio-political transformations of the past half-century but also a longer meta-textual tradition of its epic tales, mythical figures, narratives, and national icons. Perhaps therein lies the clue to understanding his continuing stardom as the multiple iterations and extensions of his star texts locate him not only in a particular historical period but also in mythic imaginaries that go beyond socio-political transformations. As such, further analyses of the mythical resonances embodied by Bachchan's star persona may offer clues not only to his screen success over an unprecedented period of time but also to the wider study of stars and stardom in the country.

5 IMPACT ON CONTEMPORARY CULTURAL PRODUCTION

After nearly half a century, Bachchan's performances and film texts have become master texts of their own, informing contemporary cinema, including his own films, in guises of *hommage*, imitation, and/or subversion. He continues to impact upon film narratives and styles, thc formations of star texts and the cinematic performances of other stars. Moreover, the star casts a long shadow on cultural production in both high and popular spheres, including art, literature, and fashion as well as other cultural artefacts including comic books, graphic novels, and animation clips. As such, it is necessary to examine Bachchan's effect not only on Indian cinema but also on wider cultural production.

Predictably, Bachchan's influence on Indian cinema is enormous, complicated, and multifaceted. Stars attempt to emulate aspects of his on-screen appearance and performance, replicate his narratives, and reaffirm their own stardom by association, and try to out-do his success by starring in remakes of his films, such as *Don* (2006), with Shah Rukh Khan as the eponymous lead, and *Agneepath* (2012) with Hrithik Roshan reprising the role of Dinanath Vijay Chauhan, in an attempt to capitalise on earlier successes. Moreover, while filmmakers in the 1970s and 1980s created star vehicles for Bachchan, a new generation of filmmakers, who grew up consuming those films are now actively referencing the star and his films in stylistic, aesthetic, and narrative terms. Films like *Main Hoon Na* (I Am Here for You, 2004) and *Gangs of Wasseypur* (2012) draw on the star's persona and provide insights into how Bachchan continues to influence filmmaking. Finally, the star's screen appearances as himself in films ranging from *Chhoti Si Baat* (1975) to *English Vinglish* (2012) indicate a conscious and deliberate strategy to reinforce his star status over the full period of his career to date.

The star in and of cinema

By 1980, Bachchan's stardom had become a template of sorts and there appeared little choice for later stars but to incorporate aspects of his performance, style, and aesthetic, albeit with limited success: Jackie Shroff drew on the brooding, angry young man persona; Anil Kapoor tried to combine elements of comedy with action; Mithun Chakravarty delivered action and dancing in a single package; while Sanjay Dutt attempted to blend action with emotional vulnerability. These stars were tall and muscular, with long hair, mannerisms and roles that echoed and evoked the superstar. However, despite varying degrees of critical and commercial success, none was able to emulate his success. They were also, at least in part, hampered by Bachchan's continued and predominant screen presence, and were pitched in direct competition.

However, as Bachchan's career began to decline in the late 1980s, a generation of shorter, softer stars began to carve out new roles, primarily as romantic leads, which was one of the areas that Bachchan's persona had not fully encompassed. However, new stars like Salman Khan and Aamir Khan still included strands of action and comedy, and neither had a compelling enough star biography to tap into or reflect the zeitgeist. That vacuum would be filled by Shah Rukh Khan's arrival on film screens in 1992, with a string of modest films. No other star has evoked, subverted, and challenged Bachchan's star text and persona with as much success as Khan.

Veteran actress Amrita Singh who had known the star from his childhood in Delhi notes that 'Shah Rukh wanted to be Bachchan' (quoted in Chopra 2007). Khan's star biography resonates with characteristics drawn from Bachchan's, including his 'odd' looks and 'early days of struggle', and highlighting his 'outsider' status in the film industry, despite his familiarity if not intimacy with the country's political and cultural circles. Echoing Bachchan's night on the streets of Mumbai, Khan too spent a night on the city's streets, announcing at dawn that he would one day 'rule the town' (Chopra 2007: 71). Unlike the older star, however, Khan's narrative is rooted in romance with the actor arriving in Mumbai not to seek success but find his girlfriend (now wife). Khan's star biography thus amalgamates material ambition and romance, a powerful combination for the post-liberalisation 1990s.[1]

Khan's early film choices also reference Bachchan's screen persona with a series of roles that cast him as a 'middle-class boy' and an angry young man albeit one whose rage was fragmented into psychotic violence.[2] Khan's star biography has repeatedly highlighted his fandom, noting that he 'thought even Amitabh's bad films were good' and imitated the star in his mannerisms, looks, and dress (ibid: 2007).

At the same time, following his initial success, Khan was quick to position himself as diametrically opposite to Bachchan. Instead of the brooding intensity and elite background of the older star, Khan's star biography emphasises his middle-class upbringing and values, an open, friendly personality, and an intense loyalty to his wife and family. While Bachchan's star text rested on an incongruous juxtaposition of a screen persona of the disenfranchised 'proletariat' and a privileged personal life, Khan's parallel text seamlessly blended, especially post-1995, his personal life and screen persona (Singh 2008). A smooth synthesis of film roles and star biography made Khan 'the personification of the collective ideals and longings of a country undergoing social upheaval' (Chopra 2007: 139). As Khan's stardom grew, building on an aesthetic of stabilisation that contrasted with Bachchan's aesthetic of mobilisation, the star's persona and biography became fully intertwined: after *Dilwale Dulhaniya Le Jayenge* (*The Bravehearted Will Take the Bride*, 1995, popularly known as *DDLJ*), Khan would become the Raj – the name of characters he often played onscreen. Eschewing violence for peace-making, Khan would position himself as the opposite of Bachchan as well as the embodiment of the zeitgeist.

Unsurprisingly, given Khan's own fandom and star status, he was the obvious choice for the remake of the 1970s super-hit *Don*. The remake, if successful, would seal his star status as equal to that of the older star.[3] At the same time, the film would also revive the circulation of Bachchan's original film as well as other releases of the time, and thus prove beneficial to both.

With clever changes to the original script, the remake of *Don* was clearly constructed as a star vehicle for Khan, intended to extend his screen persona from that of the responsible father, dutiful son, and attentive lover. The film successfully draws on both strands of Khan's star persona, the 'psychotic hero' and the more dominant one, based on the 'aesthetic of mobilisation' as well as evoking Bachchan's earlier success. To achieve this seemingly contradictory set of goals, *Don* builds on SRK's ideal lover persona and shows him loyal to his lady love despite flirtations with other women, kind to children, and even engineering a family reunion for a supporter, albeit for purposes that suit him. The notion of a *doppelganger* – in the original, the crime boss is replaced by his 'good' lookalike – had allowed the earlier film the necessary moral ambiguity to conform to

Bachchan's star text but is removed in the remake. Khan's Don not only kills the innocent Vijay, but also coolly carries off an intricate series of impersonations.

While one could argue that Khan's own star persona would disqualify him from playing a murderous criminal, the remake entirely privileges Don's point of view, thus allowing the protagonist to commit numerous crimes, including murder. Furthermore, these are presented as reflections of a greater aspirational, empire-building strategy, with Don the ultimate symbol of material ambitions. As such, Don may punish 'traitors' but his actions are depicted as the result of appropriate strategic decisions. The film ends with Don as the undisputed ruler of Asia's criminal underworld, cockily declaring, 'I am the king', with the dialogue a play on Khan's name as well as his title within the industry. This declaration, at the conclusion of a star-vehicle remake, carries an extra-textual significance, relating to the earlier superstar's longevity and success. The timing of the film, co-incidentally, underscored the link between the two stars as Bachchan had played his first unambiguously 'godfather'-like role in *Sarkar*, released a few months earlier.

Roshan's *Agneepath* in 2012 was a much less successful remake, not in the least due to the flaws of the original. Roshan, born into a film family, seemed at the start of the millennium to embody all the values of the post-liberalisation, consumerist generation. From his debut film *Kaho Na Pyaar Hai* (Say That You Love Me, 2000), the actor was hailed as the next major star, although his success rate has been patchy since, with spectacular failures punctuated by some hits. His chiselled good looks, strikingly light eyes, and a buffed physique stand in complete contrast to Khan – and Bachchan's – rather ordinary looks. He played the younger son/brother in the lush family saga *K3G*, and held his own against the two veterans. However, Roshan has no coherent screen persona, and mixes and matches comedy, romance, sentimentality and action in various films. Casting him in *Agneepath* seemed an odd decision as, despite his acting skills, he doesn't have the star status required for the role. Although the remake substantially tightened the script, shedding much of the star-specific 'attractions' of the original, dramatically improved the production values, and Roshan brought much freshness and energy to the lead, the film was only moderately successful.

The remake evoked the Bachchan original as well as *Deewar*, not in the least in the casting of Priyanka Chopra as Kaali Gawde, Vijay's love interest. Chopra's looks have often been compared to Parveen Babi, who played Anita in *Deewar* and Kaali's easy intimacy with Vijay also replicates the relationship from that film. However, unlike Bachchan's *Agneepath*, where Mary and her son survive, Kaali is gunned down soon after her wedding to Vijay, echoing Anita's death in the earlier film. The remake also removes the comic sequences played by Krishnan in the original, structuring the narrative as a clearer revenge plot. It also eliminates the poorly developed, cartoonish gangsters and replaces them with the pimp and human trafficker Rauf Lala (Rishi Kapoor).

The film also reframes the urban slum as a place of solidarity despite the poverty and violent crime. In this reconfigured city, Vijay's ragtag coalition comprises a well-armed group of men, supported by a local gang of muscular *hijras*. At the same time, and perhaps indicative of a disturbing change in the public imaginary since 1990, the remake also relinquishes the visual secularism of the original, depicting the street as a primarily Hindu space, with other religions marginalised, and their overt markers driven indoors. A corollary of this reconceptualisation of the city is the reformulation of the villains, now entirely rooted in the rural landscape, not the suave, urban criminals of the original, but rather the remnants of a backward, feudal order.

The suave Kancha Cheena is replaced by a larger-than-life, psychopathic version played by Sanjay Dutt. Kancha's obsessive repetition of a verse about the eternal nature of the soul, especially in moments of violence, may be intended to signal the rise of the Hindu right wing, although its impact is minimal.[4] By framing villainy in individual terms, the remake makes space for the blamelessness of the villagers; unlike the original, the village remains inhabited at the end, with the villagers helping Vijay overcome Kancha's henchmen. The final shot of the film does not focus on a dead hero and an apocalyptic landscape, but rather on a young Vijay and his father walking off into a verdant landscape, suggesting a nostalgic attempt to reclaim a sort of prelapsarian innocence.

The remake reaffirms Bachchan's stardom but fails to extend its benefits to Roshan. Although changes in tastes and even socio-political transformations play a part in the reception of both films, at least some of the narrative failures of both versions of *Agneepath* may be attributed to the overwhelming star persona of Bachchan in the first and his absence in the latter.

However, Bachchan's stardom doesn't just loom large over other actors. It also casts a long shadow on filmmakers, especially those who grew up in the 1970s and 1980s. Although examining the full scope of his influence on cinema requires a separate study, it is important to register the extent of his continuing impact. Films like *Dev* and *Khakee* draw overtly on Bachchan's stardom as essential parts of their appeal, using him to endow the narrative with both moral force and cinematic power. At the same time, the star's influence on films that neither make an overt reference to nor cast him is more intriguing. *Main Hoon Na* and *Gangs of Wasseypur* exemplify not only the star's extraordinary influence but also the range of ways filmmakers engage with it.

Farah Khan's *Main Hoon Na*is ostensibly a tribute to the 1970 'epic' film that also inverts and updates its conventions. The family is separated not by fate but by infidelity and pride, and is eventually reunited by the efforts of a loving son. Exhorted by his dying father, Brigadier Shekhar (Naseeruddin Shah), Ram (Shah Rukh Khan) sets out to find his father's legitimate family and reunite them. Referencing Khan's star text of the hero whose best weapon is persuasion, the film requires Ram to convince his half-family to accept him. En route to this family reconciliation, he must also battle a dreaded terrorist Raghavan (Sunil Shetty). With twists and turns worthy of a Manmohan Desai-starrer, the film revisits familiar tropes: the serious elder brother who lightens up– a sort of amalgamated Amar and Anthony of *Amar Akbar Anthony*; the happy-go-lucky younger brother, Lakshman (Zayed Khan) reprising the comical Akbar. Chandni (Sushmita Sen) is named not only after Sridevi's role from the eponymous 1989 film but also evokes Zeenat Aman and Parveen Babi, who played modern, sexually empowered 'glamour girls' opposite Bachchan in the 1970s and 1980s.

The film resurrects many of the themes from Bachchan's early films: the family becomes a stand-in for the nation and its eventual reconciliation is a necessary resolution for a conflicted nation-state. Moreover, maternal approval is the main motivation for Ram's actions. The film elides vital aspects of Bachchan's star text, expecting a knowing audience to recognise the references: Khan's first appearance as a serious army officer is a nod to *Zanjeer*'s police officer; the school setting and eventual kidnap of the students evokes *Do Aur Do Paanch* (Two and Two Make Five, 1980); Ram's undercover gig as a mature student sets him up not only for costumes from the 1970s, especially Bachchan's iconic flares and printed shirts from *Bombay to Goa*, *Kasme Vade*, and *Don*, but also for comedy, mirroring Bachchan's shift from pure action dramas. Ram's 'dual' role, as the tough army officer and comical geek invoke Bachchan films like *Great Gambler*, *Satte pe Satta*, and *Shahenshah*, where he played multiple roles, each capitalising on an aspect of his star persona.

Main Hoon Na also includes multiple cinephilic references,[5] including a trip ostensibly to watch *Sholay*. Hoardings and mammoth stills of the blockbuster surround the theatre while the macho posturing of a punter in the queue parodies the often unexplained aggression of the angry young man. In the following sequence, more inter-textuality leavens the slick action with comedy: an image of Gabbar is reflected in the darkened windows of the villains' car while Ram chases the thugs in a rickshaw with Dhanno emblazoned on the back, referencing not only Basanti's horse but also the various chase sequences from the original film.[6]

On the surface, the upbeat, *Main Hoon Na* could not be more different from *Gangs of Wasseypur*, Anurag Kashyap's gritty, six-hour long, multi-generational historical saga set in India's coal belt but neither film can escape Bachchan's overwhelming presence. In Kashyap's film, the most overt influence is aesthetic, especially once the narrative shifts to the 1970s and after. Film theatres often feature in the background, and film posters form the visual backdrop of its poverty-stricken, violent small towns, the elision of narrative time and pace of life marked by a mix of old and new films that seem to occupy the public arena at the same time. Film theatres and film viewing, and their centrality to public life and as sites of desire– material, social, and sexual – are emphasised, including in a disturbing scene where a little girl begs male customers entering a theatre to take her in to see the film. Moreover, references to Bachchan abound, including an explanation by a minor character that 'revenge' is better achieved as a criminal as in *Deewar* rather than as a cop as in *Zanjeer*.

The film's masculinities are also constructed to reflect Bachchan's influence, although these constructs are complicated as the influence of and on the star was not a one-way transaction. Bachchan drew on northern non-urban mannerisms, body language, and lingo for his performances, albeit with much studied sophistication. In return, north Indian male fans, especially from non-urban areas, copied the star's on-screen mannerisms, playing out their own life stories with imitations of the actor. *Gangs of Wasseypur* brings another layer of complexity to this ritual of imitation and replication with its characters demonstrating their fandom within the narrative. The star's loose shirts, flared jeans, and overgrown hair cut in the 'Bachchan style' are imitated by both brothers, Faizal (Nawazuddin Siddiqui) and Danish (Vineet Singh). Faizal is shown to be a film fanatic, as is his sweetheart Mohsina (Huma Qureshi),[7] who is an avid Bachchan fan, and their romance is replete with references to the star. Their initial meeting is accompanied by a song from *Muqaddar ka Sikandar* that sends Faizal into a romantic fantasy. Their matching Ray Ban sunglasses in Faizal's fantasy are a sly reference to Bachchan's early use of the brand onscreen as well as to the ways cinephilia informs real-life interactions.

Furthermore, the film's historic trajectory exemplifies the ways in which Bachchan's star persona engaged with representations of provincial masculinities over time:

> The Bachchan hero is the first generation consumer, having recently broken the shackles of the savings-regime of the FYP political economy. He is as much anti-statist in taking the law into his own hands, as announcing the beginnings of a consumerist agenda (Srivastava 2013: 43).[8]

The film's comprehensive engagement with India's history and cinephilia, and its conscious evocation of the ways Bachchan's stardom impacted upon articulations of masculinities amongst non-metropolitan men makes it a nuanced articulation of the link between cinema and reality, as well as a fascinating study of the link between the star, his fans, and real life.

Finally, star status is also reinforced by films in which the star appears as himself using the on-screen appearance to bolster his off-screen mystique, glamour, and status by the on-screen adoration and awestruck reactions that such appearances receive. Bachchan's on-screen appearances as himself date back to *Chhoti si Baat* (A Small Thing, 1975) and *Gol Maal (Chaos, 1979)*, and continue today with films like *Ramji Londonwale* (2005) and *Bol Bachchan* (Speak Bachchan, 2012).

Bachchan's first on-screen appearance as himself in *Chhoti si Baat*, coincides with the first phase of his stardom and the shedding of his middle-class screen persona. The film codes his stardom in two distinct ways: a prominent hoarding of Bachchan's *Zameer* (Conscience, 1975) looms above the bus stop where the film's protagonists meet; and Bachchan appears, as himself, in a brief scene at the personality development centre, to consult Colonel Singh (Ashok Kumar) about some tax papers. As both films had the same producer and were shot at the same time, the hoarding functions as a clever bit of cross-advertising, and signals the star's visibility and omnipresence in popular imagination. His appearance in Colonel Singh's centre is an affirmation of the centre's success within the film for a doubting Arun (Amol Palekar) while it also reinforces the 'realism' of the film's middle-class cinema aesthetic (Poduval 2012). Moreover, Arun's star-struck reaction reasserts for the film's characters, as well as the viewers, the mystique and glamour of the star.

The device is repeated in *Gol Maal* with a slight difference: Ram (Amol Palekar) runs into the star outside a film studio where *Jurmana* (Forfeit, 1979) is being shot. The two films were being made by Hrishikesh Mukherjee at the same time. Ram shakes the star's hand, his star struck demeanour encoding the real-life fan's gaze. Later in the film, Ram fantasises about replacing Bachchan as the biggest star, placing himself not only in the star's on-screen roles but also imagining his fandom. Ram's sequences set up a puzzle box where off-screen realities and cinematic references are fused into one compact on-screen bundle, underpinned only by the presence of the superstar.[9]

Post-2000, Bachchan's on-screen appearances as himself have subtly changed. Although they continue to fulfil the functions described above, they are also coded to reassert the star's dominance. After the collapse of ABCL, the star's appearances in advertisements, live shows, and public ceremonies increased substantially, in part as a means of generating income. At the same time, the *KBC* persona of the benevolent patriarch validating the twinned ideals of national pride and capitalist aspirations meant he could be called upon to encourage or reaffirm the success of film characters. In the final sequence of *Ramji Londonwale*, Bachchan appears to 'inaugurate' Ramji's (R. Madhavan) much dreamed-of restaurant. His arrival is marked by all the trappings of a superstar, with a luxury car accompanied by security. The camera focuses on the star's glossy shoes, and then his hand, before pulling back to reveal his face, an entrance that replicates the highly stylised conventions of his earlier films. Ramji's open-mouthed wonder is highlighted and the aspirations of the wider nation reinforced by the star exclaiming that 'Sab kuch mumkin hai' (Everything is possible). At the same time, there is an overt and new acknowledgment of the star's power as well as of the visual connections that binds him to his fans.[10]

Other recent appearances work on similar principles, although *Bol Bachchan* not only references the star's persona in its title but also features the star's son Abhishek as Abbas Ali. Bachchan himself only appears in an 'item song' featuring some of his memorable dialogues ineptly performed by Abbas and Prithviraj (Ajay Devgan). The star himself corrects and completes their efforts. The song ends with Bachchan addressing the audience directly to explain that 'Hum film mein hain nahin, sirf naam hai hamara: Bachchan' (I am not in the film; it just carries my name: Bachchan). Although the song sequence, title, and multitude of narrative references, reinforce the star's continued stardom, this comes at a cost: Bachchan's son has been unable to attain similar success and much of his stardom is based on his real-life relationship with his father.

A final mention must be made of the star's appearance in *English Vinglish* as the unnamed stranger who helps Shashi

(Sridevi) during a plane journey. His ability to command attention from the stewardesses as well as his confidence in dealing with the US immigration process – a dreaded experience for most Indians – demonstrate not only his stardom but his assumed off-screen role as the guide and mentor of the nation. His translation of an English film for Shashi, complete with voice changes and special effects is played for comedy, and to affirm his acting expertise. Most importantly, he becomes the familiar, anchoring presence at a moment when Shashi is feeling acutely dislocated and isolated. The star not only offers his generosity within the narrative but serves as an extra-textual reminder of the ways his media images are points of familiarity and comfort for expatriates, immigrants, and travelling Indians.

Darśana, and a single glimpse of the star

In discussing Bachchan's impact on cinema, we must consider one final film: Anurag Kashyap's short film *Murabba*[11] (Preserve), released as part of *Bombay Talkies* (2013) to mark the centenary of Indian cinema. The short explores trans-generational cinephilia, the attraction and power of stardom, and the relationship between stars and their fans. The film opens in Allahabad, the star's natal city, where Vijay (Vineet Kumar Singh), in an echo of the small-time cons from early Bachchan films, makes money by persuading pilgrims to take *darśana* of a powerful ascetic. His long hair, slightly flared, faded jeans, and check shirt are reminiscent of Bachchan's iconic 1970s appearances. The initial sequence incorporates other familiar narrative tropes: the child who informs Vijay of his father's illness, the ailing but loving father, and the supportive mother. The father (Sudhir Pandey) recalls that his own father asked him to carry a jar of honey to Dilip Kumar so the star could bless it by dipping his finger into it. Blessed by the star, the honey had extended the ailing man's life for years. He wants Vijay to fulfill similar task: carry a single preserved gooseberry (*murabba*) to Bachchan, to be tasted and returned as a cure for his illness.

The use of food, to be blessed and returned, is an overt reference to the Hindu concept of *prasad*, the devotional offering made to a deity, and then consumed by devotees. *Murabba* links the practice of fandom to ritual practices of *darśana* by pilgrims who undertake long and arduous expeditions to sacred sites. Vijay's journey to Mumbai, his difficulties, and the prolonged wait outside the star's home, the final 'summoning' by the icon himself, and his entry past the gates to finally see his idol all replicate the motifs, rituals, and stages of a religious pilgrimage.

The film also links Vijay to the star's screen persona, narratively echoing the 1970s tropes of the dangerous city: he is conned by a taxi driver, told off by the guards at the star's home, and eventually finds himself penniless, hungry, and without lodging. Yet the narrative also subtly marks the difference between Vijay's reality and the films he remembers: he has a 'return ticket' that will take him home, and the only obstacle to his return is his desire to fulfil his father's wishes. Bachchan's screen persona and the fandom surrounding him are also encoded visually: Vijay's bright red shirt recalls Bachchan's uniform in *Coolie* and a glimpse of Haji Ali is a reminder of that film's climax, as well as of the emotive secularism of an earlier era. The film underlines Bachchan's ubiquitous presence in the country's public imagination and its streets: Vijay's taxi drives past an endless row of hoardings, each showing the star endorsing various consumer products; outside the star's house, he runs into a star lookalike who makes a living posing with fans; posters, hoardings, and a seeming ascetic on a bicycle decorated with what appears to be an altar to the star reinforce Vijay's participation in an all-encompassing fandom. Indeed, so ubiquitous is the star's presence that a homeless Vijay finds himself sleeping on a discarded hoarding displaying the star's face.

A tribute to the star and stardom. Vineet Kumar Singh in *Murabba: Bombay Talkies* (2013)

The film also highlights a sort of subaltern solidarity, reminiscent of Bachchan's early films: Vijay is helped by a street-vendor and then one of the star's guards. The film's minor characters are identified as outsiders, like the star's on-screen roles and off-screen star text as aspirants. By clearly identifying them, by language and narrative information, as north Indians from the Hindi heartland, the film further reinforces the link between the star's biography, his screen persona, and the identification of his fans with both.

Vijay's travails are finally rewarded with a meeting with his idol. In a Bachchan film, the scene's soundtrack would require temple bells, *bhajans* or other devotional material; for Vijay however, the star's appearance is accompanied by fragments of his most famous dialogues. His quest completed, Vijay heads home with the remaining *murabba*, only to have a passenger in the train break the jar, and another to inadvertently step on the remnants. But unlike in the films, Vijay cannot and does not resort to violence. Instead, he procures another jar and gooseberry to fool his father, even carefully biting into the replacement fruit to imitate the teeth marks left by the star.

His return home is anti-climactic as his father challenges him on his tale, confessing that on his own trip to the city, the honey had been contaminated by ants. Repulsed, Dilip Kumar had refused to dip his finger and the father had dipped his own finger into the honey instead and lied about it. The film contrasts Bachchan's obvious relish in tasting the *murabba* with the earlier star's disdain. It also positions Bachchan as the more generous star, while also validating Vijay's quest in contrast to his father's futile one.

The film ends on a cryptic note: the father ruminates on the nature of fandom and cinephilia, noting that 'Achaar ki botal mein murabba nahin rakhna chahiye' (One should not keep sweet preserve in a pickle jar). Vijay, recounting his tale to his friend, nonchalantly explains that Bachchan had 'blessed him', but follows it up with his father's quote, leaving the viewer questioning the nature of fandom, the illusion required to maintain it, and the inexplicable link between a fan and the star.

Although a detailed discussion is beyond the scope of this study, a brief exploration of *darśana* is crucial as *Murabba* actively and consciously employs its mechanisms, and because similar mechanisms of viewing and transformation also inform other films and visual arts. *Darśana* is not merely mobilised by cinema to replicate older forms of *seeing* performance, but to reconstitute the practice itself. As Vasudevan notes, 'the localised deployment of filmic techniques in the micro-narration of a scene – editing, shot-distance and angle, camera, movement, lighting, sound elements – alert us to how characters and spectators are being cinematically positioned in relation to the *darshanic*' (2000: 140). Indeed, cinematic activation of *darśana* in culturally specific viewing practices – intra- and extra-cinematically – can be particularly useful in understanding the ways a spectator savours cinema, and finds both identification and aspiration in film stars. Although the role of *darśana* in the construction of star texts has yet to be comprehensively investigated, it is not too daring to suggest that the visual connection forged by the *darśana* is especially notable for the way it can mobilise the knowing spectator, claiming an affectionate intimacy on behalf of the star not only in specific filmic moments but also over a range of filmic texts in a star's trajectory.[12]

Although Prasad and Vasudevan identify *darśana* as a key principle of Hindi cinema, it has generally been applied in a very narrow sense, with detailed technical analysis that does not necessarily encompass the cultural and philosophical roots of the viewing practice.[13] Both scholars locate the mechanisms and practice of *darśana* as hegemonic affirmations of power: Prasad situates the practice as 'a relation of perception within the public traditions of Hindu worship, especially in the temples, but also in public appearances of monarchs and other elevated figures' (1998: 75). Similarly Vasudevan notes that in *darśana*, the devotee is permitted to behold the image of the deity, and is privileged and benefited by this permission, in contrast to a concept of looking that assigns power to the beholder by reducing the image to an object of the look'(2000: 139).

Such a view ignores the complexity where 'a mutually complicit merging of subject-object positions is a necessary requisite' as the act of 'being seen' by the deity allows for an internal transformation and the experience of the divine (Coorlawala 1996: 24). Moreover, solely focusing on aspects of humility practised by the devotee in *darśana*, ignores

> the entire range of intimate and ordinary acts as an important part of ritual... Hindu worship reveals not only an attitude of honour but also an attitude of affection in the range of ritual act and gesture utilized in the treatment of the image (Eck 1996: 47).

A culturally grounded reading of *darśana* suggests quite a different process and does not necessitate homage as given to a superior: 'because the image is a form of the Supreme Lord, it is precisely the image that facilitates and enhances the close relationship of the worshipper and God and makes possible the deepest outpourings of emotions in worship' (Eck 1996: 46). Instead, an

> image of a deity in the temple, a *moorti*, remains just another icon, until the worshipper is transformed in its presence. Without at least *one viewer to taste* (even when that viewer is The Unseen Witness), *there cannot be a performance* (my italics, Coorlawala 2003: 38).

Under this conceptual construct, just as an image has no divine power without a worshipper, a performance – or indeed a star – cannot exist without the viewer.

Indeed, *darśana* is a 'subjective experience implying a heightened sense of awareness. For devotees blessed with the faculty of subtle sight the image is a sentient being, but for those with the limited faculty of gross sight it remains a lifeless statue'(Bennett 1990: 190). Moreover, the relationship between the devotee and the divine is not constituted of a hierarchy, but rather one that implies an intimate complicity and familiarity: 'An observer who aligns with the dominating male gaze which claims possession, or which criticizes and separates, is unlikely to experience transformation' (Coorlawala 1996: 24). Instead, the complicity between the subject and the object functions to entirely remove the voyeuristic gaze, as *darśana* 'together with its aesthetic equivalent, the concept of performer as *darpana* (mirror), involve a reversal of the power structures of voyeurism' (ibid.).[14] The *darśanic* gaze not only establishes a subject-object complicity, it erases the power hierarchy with the performer/mirror reflecting aspects of the subject's own self. As such, the purpose of *darśana* is not to pay homage but rather to experience a transformation that is shared by both the icon and the viewer.

In a country where film viewing is considered a passionate social, familial, and communal activity, spectators not only go to 'see' their favourite film stars, but often phrase the ritual of film viewing in more familiar terms – of 'meeting' the stars. Although

Prasad *et al* have noted that *darśana* is used colloquially not only for deities but other personages, the term is also popularly used by north Indian Hindi speakers for seeing friends, colleagues, and other intimates. Indeed, *Murabba* consciously and credibly uses the term: Vijay's quest is coded as the star's *darśana*, while the setting of the Kumbh Mela and Vijay's job reinforces the link between religious and secular, between cinephilia and devotion. Moreover, *darśana* functions as a nuanced mechanism for the visual interaction between intra-filmic deity, Bachchan, and the characters, especially Vijay, as well as forging a visual and emotional connection between the on-screen stars and the spectator.[15]

Murabba most overtly mobilises this spectator-star connection when Vijay finally sees Bachchan. The shot sequence recreates the entrance of the devotee into a temple, with the focus on Vijay's face as he veers between disbelief, awe, fear, and gratitude. Initially, the camera only shows Bachchan obliquely, with each reverse shot moving the star more firmly into Vijay's view. The low-angle camera positions Bachchan in iconic terms. Yet this is no 'despotic spectacle' of a king being adored by subservient subjects, but rather each reverse shot draws Vijay closer to his idol, emphasising the momentary but powerful intimacy that marks a key moment of transformation in Vijay's 'internal' self. The *darśanic* is mobilised here as an extra-filmic acknowledgment of the spectator by the star whose gaze acknowledges both the presence and importance of the spectator.

At the same time, the sequence utilises filmic techniques, camera angles, sound, and editing, to emphasise the egalitarian complicity between the spectator and the star. Here the edit subtly reinforces the transformation, in the performer, the intra-cinematic audience as well as the spectator, that *darśana* requires and produces: 'The camera's invitation to gaze through the deity's (or star's) eyes heightens the experience of the reciprocality of *darshan*, closing an experiential loop to evoke (in a characteristically Indic move) an underlying unity' (Lutgendorf 2004: 11). Vijay's insistence that the star taste the *murabba* in his presence not only evokes the tradition of cajoling, even hectoring, a personalised deity, but also gives visual materiality to the symbolic ritual when *prasad* is presented and 'tasted' by the deity. Bachchan's obvious relish, as he licks his fingers clean, signals the star's acceptance, acknowledgment, and appreciation of not only the offering but of Vijay's – and by extension – his fans' devotion.

Yet the film also differentiates between the spiritual transformation wrought by *darśana* of a deity and its cinephilic illusion. By the time Vijay returns home, he is ready to demonstrate, if not a 'real' transformation, then at least an illusion of it. While his earlier interactions with his father were in a series of reverse shots, with Vijay's worried face looming above the ailing man, the interaction between the two is shot entirely in medium and medium close-ups, the camera asserting Vijay's new-found equality with the older man, now united by their interaction with, and knowledge of stars. The film seems to suggest that although stars may not be deities performing miracles, they can offer a semblance of change that in turn can be replicated on a smaller scale by their fans, thus extending the cycle of cinematic illusions ever further.[16]

Thus the activation of *darśana* in cinema offers an intimate pleasure, generated by the ways in which cinematic and extra-cinematic techniques are mobilised. This pleasure is enhanced not only by certain filmic techniques but by the spectator actively engaging with extra-filmic information, including specific parallel texts of stars, the socio-political context of the narrative as well as comprehensive meta-textual references to epics, heroes, and historical events and figures. Indeed it would not be entirely misplaced to speak of visual *connections* as opposed to visual interactions as crucial to *darśanic* viewing practices, where the spectator is not only actively acknowledged by the stars on screen, but allowed to forge an active connection between the on-screen images, off-screen materiality of the stars, and the consumer of the same.

Beyond the screen

Given the star's extensive career, there are few forms of cultural production in India that are not imbricated with the star's presence – conscious and unconscious.

Since the 1980s, for example, literary products have drawn on Bachchan's screen image and star text for piquancy, a sense of 'realism' and authenticity, and for ways of exploring the philosophical and political anxieties of the nation. He is important in Vikas Swarup's 2006 novel, *Q & A* (adapted into the film, *Slumdog Millionaire* 2008), with the young characters enamoured of his screen persona. Although the star never appears in the novel or the film, his presence in the imaginations of characters and the viewer is crucial to the narrative. The star functions as the embodiment of the characters' aspirations and dreams while the phenomenal success of his *KBC* serves as the main plotting device.

Similarly, Shashi Tharoor's 1992 satirical novel, *Show Business*, is based entirely on Bachchan's star biography. The novel is framed in a sequence of 'flashbacks' as the protagonist battles for life after an on-set accident, drawing on the real-life incident and the public hysteria that gripped the nation afterwards. Shobha De's *Starry Nights* (1991) uses the actor's much-rumoured affair with Rekha as its primary plot device, with multiple elements of popular fiction and an outlandish plot that includes domestic violence, multiple lovers, arms dealers, and an improbable climax. Vikram Chandra's monumental cinephilic tribute *Red Earth, Pouring Rain* (1995) is more subtle in its evocation of the star. In one memorable sequence, Ganesha asserts the primacy of life, a point accepted by mortal and immortal characters within the scene as well as the narrator and by extension, the writer:

And so, in the time left to us before the hour of storytelling, we watched *Amar Akbar Anthony*, and fine feast it was; replete and nourished, I leapt up to my typewriter, and typed, and laughed as the words echoed over the growing crowd on the maidan ... (1995: 124).

However, it is Salman Rushdie's *The Satanic Verses* that makes the most elaborate use of Bachchan's stardom, employing an array of film texts, biography, and film-press gossip in an exuberant mix of high-low art. Rushdie's Gibreel Farishta is an amalgam of real stars and fantasy but Bachchan's imprint is impossible to miss:

For over a decade and a half he had represented, to hundreds of millions of believers in that country, in which, to this day, the human population outnumbers the divide by less than three to one, the most acceptable, and instantly recognisable, face of the Supreme' (1998: 16–17).

The novel, often overshadowed by political controversy, is a reminder of star's impact on the nation and its imagination.

Unsurprisingly, Bachchan has also inspired visual arts and artists. In 2012, the *B Seventy* exhibition at Mumbai's Nehru Centre brought together some of India's major artists in a *festschrift* of sorts for the star. The works included in the exhibition reaffirm the star's influence, mark a point of engagement between popular and high cultures in the country, and illustrate the variety of aesthetic, political, and philosophical engagements with the star and his persona.

Amitabh Bachchan Chair, a 2002 mixed media/bois work by Anjolie Ela Menon, features the star in a painted wooden chair, his face and upper torso comprising the backrest and lower body covering the seat. Along the sides, a black and white border echoes old film reels. While the star is costumed in his iconic white trousers, his bright yellow shirt and blue jacket appear incongruous. His hand lies in his lap, a gun posed over his crotch. The dark hair and white beard are reminders of the star's look in *Mohabbatein*. Although the face shows few wrinkles, the star's mien as youthful as ever, the eyes seem pensive, even exhausted. The lavender/pink background that bleeds into the chair's legs and sides is reminiscent of the 'bazaar art' aesthetic and clashes with the blue of the chair's arms, queering any assertion of stereotypical masculinity. This piece simultaneously signals the star's ubiquity and demythologises him: despite the iconic costume and prop, this is no superstar but rather an ageing man, slumped rather than simply seated.

Sanjay Bhattacharya's *Up Above the World* places a towering Bachchan in his costume from *Bunty aur Babli* (Bunty and Babli 2005), alongside some of India's best-known historic monuments including the Taj Mahal and the Qutab Minar. The star's jean-clad legs, like monumental trees, seem to reach directly into the ground beneath. The Taj Mahal shows through the translucent legs, making the star seem larger yet more ephemeral than the stone monuments around him. A bright yellow sun looms at his shoulder, forming the pinnacle of the Qutab Minar. Yet the backdrop for the star is plain, formed of dull earth tones against which his lush chocolate jacket and red scarf are highlighted. The painting seems to place the star as one of the many historic monuments of India, at once towering, rooted in the country's identity, and yet somehow isolated and beyond human.

Sculptor Arzan Khambatta's *The Throne* depicts the star's *KBC* persona. Dressed in a suit, slouched on a tall bar stool, the figure is shorn of any facial identifier. However, the overgrown hair and preternaturally long legs folding into the chair mean that there is no mistaking the actor's lean frame. The figure's posture signals both arrogance and ease, reminiscent more of Vijay's body language in *Deewar* than the studied affability that the actor adopted for KBC, collapsing four decades of audience memories into a single idealised frame of reference.

Finally, Suneel Mamdapur's *Star* evokes publicity stills from *Don*. The running figure startles a flock of pigeons, sending

Subhrajit Kar

Arzan Khambatta's *The Throne* for B Seventy exhibition (2012)

Suneel Mamdapur's *Star* for B Seventy exhibition (2012)

them flying across and seemingly out of the canvas. His patterned vest and posture are recognisable from Bachchan's iconic eponymous role. The backdrop features four similar figures placed to seemingly recede into the distance; the familiar skyline of Mumbai can be perceived through their outlines that appear as cut-outs in the yellow backdrop. Mamdapur locates Bachchan's screen persona firmly in the urban experience, eliding the actor and the city into a single evocation of energetic, even frenetic dreams, that continue to influence cultural producers of the country.

A brief mention must also be made of the street art that is emerging as a point of contact between contemporary art and the country's declining tradition of hand-painted film hoardings. Muralist Ranjit Dahiya of the Bollywood Art Project celebrated Indian cinema's centenary with giant paintings across Mumbai, including a mammoth version of Bachchan in *Deewar*, painted on a wall near Bandra's Mehboob Studios. Nor is the production of homages in street art limited to the urban centres: Rajkapoor Chitera, an Allahabad-based artist is one among many who produce works that echo and reflect Bachchan's stardom and

Ranjit Dahiya for Bollywood Art Project

form an intriguing point of engagement between fandom and popular art production. These works seem to be both an extension as well as an evolution of the many 'bazaar' images of earlier years and thus occupy a potentially exciting space between high and popular art.

Recent shifts in technology have also impacted on the ways in which culture is produced and consumed and nowhere is this more apparent than in the short animation clips and graphic novels. While many of the short animation clips are produced as parodies by television channels and even fans, and focus on subverting and spoofing key scenes from Bachchan's films for comic and, at times, political effect, there is also a move towards revisiting and revising some of the actor's classic films for other media.

The classic *Sholay* was reissued as a graphic novel in 2014, the new medium bringing an aesthetic freshness to the story. The graphic novel was accompanied by a series of mobile versions of animated clips from the movie, extending both the range of media and technological forms of circulation of the star's image. A second graphic novel titled *Gabbar* from the same group explores the film villain's 'backstory', drawing on the narrative conventions of injustice and revenge that were hallmarks of the angry young man era. It must be noted that the appearance of the star in comic book format is not new: the short-lived Supremo comics in the 1980s were endorsed by the star and drew on popular tropes from his films.

Moreover, developing technologies have been central to the continued ubiquity of the star in the popular imaginary. Bachchan's stardom was initially bolstered by his songs filling air time on short-wave radio, while his face dominated the film press, fanzines, and 'bazaar art' products, such as posters, calendars, matchboxes, and fireworks. Meanwhile, the introduction of video cassettes and the extension of television reception in the country throughout the 1980s extended the circulation of Bachchan's films beyond and outside the cinema halls. The arrival of satellite television in the 1990s and, with it, the need for increased volumes of local content introduced younger generations of spectators to his early work, expanding his fan base, and reaffirming the strength of his stardom.

Indeed, the particular role played by song sequences in the construction of stardom must be noted, especially its role in increasing consumption and distribution of star images.[17] The circulation of song sequences as audio and audio-visual products independent of the film has long been a hallmark of Indian cinema. Technological advances including television, video cassettes, and DVDs have exponentially enhanced the reach and range of the song. For Bachchan, these song compilations were especially effective during the 1990s, during the time of his self-proclaimed hiatus and during the years when his films were failing commercially. Access to older beloved songs on television, radio as well as on video cassettes and DVDs, ensured the continuing presence of his image in popular media. These collections bridged time, with nostalgia providing a link between the star and his fans until the star reinvented his screen persona.[18] Moreover, stage shows often built around beloved song sequences have provided an ongoing point of emotional and physical interaction between the star and his fans, a form astutely utilised by Bachchan, especially during his low phase in the 1990s.

Finally, Bachchan has long been an active participant in new technologies, employing multiple platforms to communicate directly with his fans, with a dedicated blog, Facebook page, and an active Twitter account. He was an early adopter of social media, and effectively presents the illusion of interacting with his fans through personalised updates, behind-the-camera photographs from various sets, and photographs of his 'normal' life. In combination with his public appearances and on-screen roles, these continually and consistently fulfil a marketing function for the star and his films, and reaffirm his ongoing engagement with his fans. Although a detailed analysis of the role of social media, new technologies and stardom, especially as employed by Indian film stars, and specifically Bachchan, is beyond the scope of the current study, it is important to note that the star continues to control, develop, and extend his stardom in new and interesting ways.

6 CONCLUSION

Bachchan's stardom is of such enduring longevity and exercises such an influence on contemporary culture in India that it seems curious that more studies have not focused on the complete period of his stardom to date. Although there has been, as noted, ground breaking work on some aspects of Bachchan's stardom, the research for this current study not only exposed the lacunae in the study of Indian cinema but also of its stars and their role on cultural production in and outside the country. Indeed, further study is required to locate Bachchan within the industry as well as to examine specific aspects of stardom in India's commercial cinema and his contribution to those conventions. Further examinations of not only Bachchan but also other Indian, and indeed all non-Western stars, and their stardom are necessary to understand the phenomenon of stars and stardom across the globe.

As Shingler notes,

> scholarship on stars within film studies continues to advance along two distinct lines: how stars work (e.g., their working methods, financial and contractual arrangements, degree of agency and professional practices), on the one hand, and how stars act or perform, on the other (2012: 183).

Kaante (2002)

At the same time, neither of these are able to explain why some stars – working with very similar tools – are able to mobilise the fan following, develop and exert national and even transnational influence on culture and politics, as well as become a semiotic focus for national and transnational identities, desires and imaginaries. Examining the intersections of Bachchan's personal life, films, national zeitgeist, and cultural paradigms may help understand this contentious issue: the elusive quality that mysteriously transforms a cinematic performance into one imbued with popular success and meaning. For this, further study is required of not only how stars work within the industry or how they act and perform but also how their cinematic appearances interact with larger cultural and social concerns and, more importantly, the ways in which they are received by their fans.

Although the current study briefly discusses how Bachchan's screen persona drew on, reflected, and informed a particular kind of subaltern, non-metropolitan masculinity, further examination of its contribution to representations of gender, not only in the star's films but to ideals of masculinities, is required. Moreover, the construction of this masculinity – which has been partially discussed by scholars including Derné (2000), Jain (2007), Mazumdar (2007), and others – needs further study, especially through lenses that draw on intersections of class, caste, gender, sexuality, and geo-cultural locations. Without acknowledging, and indeed accepting, the intersectionality of identity formation and representations in cinema, any study of Bachchan, other stars, or indeed stardom, will remain incomplete.

An examination of masculinities as embodied, represented, and subverted by Bachchan in his cinema also leads to larger questions of gender and the representation of women in commercial Hindi cinema, and how this has been transformed, both as a result of social, economic, and political changes in the country and due to the star's overwhelming embodiment of an extreme heterosexualised, aggressive masculinity. Similar questions also arise regarding queering, not only at the source in Bachchan's presentation and representation of masculinities on screen but also in regard to the ways these cinematic texts are consumed, appropriated, and reproduced over time and space. This suggests a rich vein to mine, the exploration of the distinctive representations of genders and sexualities in non-Western cinemas and how these are simultaneously affirmed, reasserted, and subverted by film stars, thus opening the space for conceptualising multiple forms of gendered and sexual identities.[1]

Moreover, further examination of the technical practices deployed to construct Bachchan's on-screen persona is also required, especially as these have been replicated, albeit with much less success, by other stars. This includes study of the early fetishist markers of costume and mise-en-scène that came to be identified with his film performances, including the white suits, bomber jackets, and high-gloss shoes that were often shown in slow camera pans and emphasised by extreme camera angles. Although these conventions of using camera, sound, and editing to highlight Bachchan's monumentality developed primarily over the first ten years of his career, they have been replicated and referenced by filmmakers both while filming the star himself, as well as in an effort to associate other male stars, including

Feroz Khan, Anil Kapoor, Jackie Shroff, Sanjay Dutt in the 1980s, as well as 'action' stars, including Ajay Devgan, Hrithik Roshan and, Bachchan's own son, Abhishek, in the 1990s and 2000s with his success.

Focus on these technical elements could help explain how these have been employed to construct, maintain, and reinvent Bachchan's on-screen presence to reaffirm established aspects of his star persona, as well as to challenge and subvert them as part of his reinventions over time. At the same time, the use of cinematic techniques meant to emphasise Bachchan's stardom may also raise questions of why and how these same conventions were not as effective when applied to other male stars. A comparative look at these aspects of the construction of Bachchan's screen persona may offer insights into the extensive interactions between cinematic techniques, a star's physicality, his performance, and larger questions of stardom.

The current study has also been unable to examine his appeal and fandom in markets outside India or the way his stardom intersects with globalised realities, ensuring his success in certain markets while he experiences near-invisibility in the 'West'. In part this invisibility in Western markets may be attributed to the dearth of starring roles available to non-white actors, especially those with significant fan followings in their own primary markets. As such, playing second fiddle to a Western star may seem to lower their star status and value, and perhaps, given the aspects of post coloniality, may even be detrimental.[2] Seen in this light, Bachchan's blink-and-you-miss-him appearance in Baz Luhrmann's 2013 extravaganza *The Great Gatsby* is not only unusual but also intriguing for the ways in which his larger-than-life persona aligns with the film's over-the-top aesthetic. Moreover, his race-bending role as Meyer Wolfsheim hints at interesting ideas of stardom, ethnicity, and identity that are yet to be explored.

Bachchan is not only a household name in India but also draws on a fanatic following in places as disparate as South

Africa, Kazakhstan, and Egypt. As Shah Rukh Khan noted on an NDTV panel on the globalisation of Bollywood, 'Every Indian is Amitabh Bachchan in Egypt.'[3] Outside of India, Bachchan's screen image not only traverses time and space but provides an imaginary alternative for constructions of modernity. With a seamless conflation of his personal life and his film roles, and shorn of the political complexities that inform his stardom in India, and perhaps due to the lack of parallel texts created and circulated by film press and fan magazines, he is seen as a model of postcolonial, modern masculinity, combining political resistance with recognisable family values. His screen narratives of social, political, economic oppression resonate with audiences beyond Indian borders, his screen persona echoing the aspirations of people who wish to simultaneously possess and experience a capitalist, Westernised modernity, while retaining their emotional connections with their family, society, and cultural norms. Discussing fandom in Nigeria, Larkin notes that 'For Hausa viewers, Indian films offer images of a parallel modernity to the West, one intimately concerned with the changing basis of social life, but rooted in conservative cultural values' (1997: 410). A similar point has been made regarding audiences in the Middle East and North Africa: 'This could be because such films deal with topics similar to those in Arab films, that is, ideal family behaviour' (Mellor *et al.* 2011: 111). There is a strong argument to be made for international fans recognising culturally resonant tropes and codes and finding comfort in similar cultural norms and values. At the same time, Bachchan's extraordinary fan following in markets in West Asia and Africa, even in countries with strong film cultures such as Egypt, where he has been repeatedly mobbed during his visits, as well as the lack of family-focused narratives in his pre-2000 films, suggests that his fans may well be looking for more than idealised family narratives and cultural tropes.

Moreover, further study is needed into Bachchan's impact on films and popular culture beyond India. What, for example, are the processes informing the transformation of Bachchan's famous *Jumma Chumma* song from *Hum* into a Hausa devotional song (discussed in Larkin 2005), or how his stardom often functions as shorthand for cinematic success, with, for example, Egyptian star Zaki Ahmed singing that he wishes to be more famous than the superstar in *Mistar Karatah* (1993). Indeed Zaki's star text also has points of contact with Bachchan's, with his screen persona often battling state corruption and structural deprivation. Zaki's fandom was also composed primarily of Egypt's working-class men, a point in common with Bachchan's Vijay persona. Comparatively studying stars such as Bachchan and Zaki may offer unique insights into not only stardom and it's constructions in non-Western cinema(s), but also into aspects of postcolonial masculinities and modernities.

Here, it is apt to revert to Khan who noted in a video tribute that he still feels like a fan and confessed to wearing Azzaro perfume because he had read that it was Bachchan's fragrance.[4] Khan's statement indicates interesting possibilities for study of Bachchan's stardom in the international context of India's 'soft power', aspects of material consumption as well as transnational fandom – with corollaries of imitation, replication, and consumption – in a globalised environment. These studies could extend also to the changes in technology that impacted upon the circulation of Bachchan's films, as well as secondary audio and visual texts, including posters, music, DVDs, and their contribute to his star text. Given the star's active role on social media platforms and his engagement with product endorsements and advertising, further analysis is needed to understand the role of stardom, especially in this age of multimedia platforms, in building and reaffirming consumerist aspirations and ideals. These lines of enquiry may help us understand not only Bachchan as a star, but also indicate how these aspects can be developed, circulated, and reproduced for other international film stars, especially those not from Hollywood.

My own research has left me with more questions than it has answered about Bachchan's star persona, as well as about the nature of stardom in general. Any clear conclusions about the star's own trajectory and status are also virtually impossible given that his screen appearances are nearly as ubiquitous as at the start of his career with three releases in 2015 and many more in varying stages of production. Shoojit Sircar's *Piku* was one of 2015's commercial and critical successes while 2016 has already seen the release of the moderately sucessful thriller, *Wazir*, with at least three more films in post-production.[5] Furthermore, he continues to strike out in new directions as demonstrated by a newly announced Disney collaboration with Graphic India to develop a fifty-two-part animated series, *Astra Force*, with a digitised Bachchan playing the protagonist, Astra – The Immortal.[6] The series is scheduled to air from 2017 on Disney India, with videogames, mobile apps, and digital comics being some of the add-ons planned for the franchise.

Moreover, it is fair to say that, despite my best efforts to separate the fan from the scholar for the purposes of this study, I have been only partially successful. As a fan, I still wait for Bachchan's new releases, albeit without the hype of 'first day, first show' of my childhood. I remain fascinated by his live appearances, although I am also able to identify – and even cringe a little – at his off- and on-screen missteps. Although the actor is no longer the infallible superstar of the 1970s and 1980s, he remains a ubiquitous and beloved presence in my imagination, memory, and life, as he no doubt does for many millions of Bachchan fans in India and across the globe.

At the same time, as a scholar, I am still unable to fully grasp the longevity and scale of his stardom. It is clear to me that the star has reinvented his star image repeatedly, each time drawing on earlier screen personas and extending them. Moreover, from the start of his career, Bachchan has kept pace with the social, economic, technological, and even narrative changes of the past half century. In addition, he has long been able to form associations with stars and filmmakers to continually revitalise his appeal and social significance, and continues to do so. For the most part, this repeated reinvention has been carried out with little acknowledgment of any anxiety on his part, although, as he explained in a recent interview, even after nearly fifty years' experience of being on film sets, 'I am intimidated almost every day.'[7] However, while I understand the process and motivation of his continual reinvention, I remain baffled by Bachchan's uncanny, and unique, ability to grasp and embody the national zeitgeist with each new incarnation. Perhaps it is this inexplicable quality that defines Bachchan as a star, and is the foundation for his lasting stardom.

NOTES

1 Introduction

1 It was probably not just Indians who voted for Bachchan but also his fans across the globe. According to Suketu Mehta, in 2005, Indian commercial cinema (Bollywood) reached a global audience of 3.6 billion people (National Geographic, 2005).

2 There are, of course, numerous fan volumes, homages and 'authorised' biographies. Of these, Dasgupta's is closest to an academic study and begins to trace the intersections between Bachchan's film texts and star biography.

3 These were especially contentious as Narendra Modi – now the Prime Minister of India – was then Chief Minister of Gujarat. In addition to belonging to the Bharatiya Janata Party, the main opposition to the Gandhi family-led Congress (I), he has also been linked to the 2002 sectarian riots in the state and was for much of the political and media elite, a pariah. Bachchan's appearance to promote the state's tourism was seen in some quarters as condoning, if not outright, supporting Modi's government.

4 This is not to disregard key works by multiple non-Indian scholars but merely intended to describe both blind spots and specific concerns that seem to inform the bulk of scholarship on Indian cinema to date.

5 As an aside, film production and scholarship in India remain dominated by members of *savarna*, or upper 'castes' which results in a significant blind spot, especially on aspects regarding representations of and consumption by the 'proletariat'. While a comprehensive discussion of *savarna*-ness is beyond the scope of this study, I am acutely aware of both the silence on the topic in film scholarship as well as my own privileged location.

6 See Dwyer on Indian film stars (2000: 118–19).

7 Barua is best known for *Devdas* (1935), made both in Bengali and Hindi, based on Sarat Chandra Chatterji's novel of the same name. The film gave Indian cinema it most enduring – and eponymous – character: 'the tragic romantic hero' (Kabir 2001). The character of Devdas was never explicitly essayed by Bachchan, whose tragic heroes have tended to be in the martial rather than romantic modes.

8 It may be argued that film stars were drawing on similar structures as earlier stars of the stage. Many theatre stars of the late nineteenth and early twentieth centuries had fan followings that are comparable to that of film stars (Hansen 2000, 2004).

9 Prasad's discussion on the rise of the male star after independence is of particular interest for its focus on the ways in which coloniality inhibits representations of masculinity prior to independence but re-inscribes a patriarchal order after it (Prasad 2004: 106–8).

10 Chapman is referring here to the writings of Rajadhyaksha.

11 I have purposely chosen the term 'commercial' to define the cinema under discussion to signal its commercial intent and purpose. Moreover 'popular' cinema carries the connotation of 'popular' vs. 'high' art, as well as issues of 'popularity' (i.e. success) that 'commercial' avoids.

12 Other scholars have grounded their analysis in psychoanalytical (Kakar 1983), Marxist dialectic (Prasad 1998) and postcolonial theories (Chakravorty 1993).

13 Despite an apparent aversion to the 'traditionalist' approach, Prasad *et al* seem to find no difficulty in deploying a reductionist version of the *darśana* theory of viewership to 'make meaning' of cinematic texts, albeit infrequently (Prasad 1998).

14 See Gandhy and Thomas (1991) for the ways in which the informal economy of cinema grew from World War II to privilege the star over other aspects.

15 Prasad 1998; also see Vitali 2008 for economics of stardom.

16 There are a few notable exceptions. See *darśana* theory as a way of reading cinematic images (Prasad 1998).

2 Birth – and Rebirth – of a Star

1 The name is explicitly referenced by *Inquilaab* and indirectly by *Main Azaad Hoon*.

2 Virdi notes that Bachchan's own narrative of his life is framed in terms of victimization, terming him the 'star victim' (2008: 234–8)

3 Cited in Bose (2006: 268).

4 Dasgupta cites a longstanding difference of opinion between Bachchan and Bhaduri over his choice of films (2006: 53) with the latter preferring the low-budget neo-realist 'parallel' cinema. Bachchan told journalist Khalid Mohammad: 'She excelled herself in a particular genre of films with Hrishikesh Mukherjee and Gulzar. Ideally, she'd like to see me in those kinds of films.' (Accessed here: http://www.sugandh.com/seema/amitabhji/khalid.html.)

5 Bachchan's first pay packet was Rs 480 a month and he also had a car. Although Bose cites these as 'hardships', the salary and perks were better than those available for many professional positions of the time.

6 Ironically, Bachchan got his film break with a voiceover in Mrinal Sen's *Bhuvan Shome* (1969).

7 Indian Institutes of Technology are a prestigious network of public institutes of higher education and have, since their founding in 1950, represented not only academic excellence but also social aspirations and mobility.

8 Raj mentions this although the rumour has circulated for years (2010: 5)

9 The photographs were taken by Bachchan's younger brother, Ajitabh, outside Calcutta's famed Victoria Memorial, who also sent them to the *Filmfare-Madhuri* talent contest, albeit without success (Bose 2006: 270).

10 The symbolic potency of this 'night on the streets' is drawn from earlier filmic canon, especially that of Raj Kapoor. 'Escape' from the footpath forms a key motif in Bachchan's early filmic texts. Finally, a similar experience forms part of Shah Rukh Khan's star biography.

11 Dasgupta and Bose have slightly different accounts of how Bachchan secured this role while Raj outright credits Mrs Gandhi for arranging it (Bose 2006: 217; Dasgupta 2006:4; Raj 2010: 5).

12 A similar path was trod by Shah Rukh Khan who took on three back-to-back negative roles in the early stages of his career, albeit with greater success.

13 Mehra had tried his hand at writing song lyrics and his four earlier films had failed to make any significant impact. Salim Khan had wanted to be an actor without much success while Javed Akhtar had been ghost-writing dialogues on mostly low-budget, forgettable films.

14 Ironically, Bhaduri acted in a short film titled 'An Angry Young Man' (1970) which was made as the 'diploma' film by an FTII student, Shamsuddin. The film starred one of Bachchan's rivals/co-stars, Shatrughan Sinha, who was also a graduate of the Film Technology Institute of India (FTII).

15 Although Jaya soon adopted her married name, I have chosen to refer to her as Bhaduri, the last name associated with her most important films and to differentiate her as a star and actor from her husband.

16 This Yash Chopra-directed film overtly deployed Bachchan's star biography. See discussion later in the chapter.

17 Dasgupta 2006. I discuss the 'epic' films in greater detail in Chapter 3.

18 For example, his supposed and long-running spat with *Stardust*, the country's major film magazine.

19 Mishra describes Bachchan's recollections as framed 'in the genre of narrative fiction' (2002: 131).

20 The Emergency lasted from 25 June 1975 to 21 March 1977. Despite Bachchan's studied naïveté, the family did not speak against the suspension of civil rights. In 1975, his father, Harivanshrai, was awarded the Padma Bhushan, one of the country's highest civilian honours. The measure confirmed the star and his family's agreement, if not collusion, with the Emergency for sections of the press.

21 See Majumdar for further discussion 'the centrality of innuendo as a particular rhetorical form of accessing and engaging stars' (2009: 11). It may be argued that Bachchan has been particularly adept at using this to his advantage.

22 She also gave at least one direct statement to the film press. In May 1982, *Cine Blitz*, a leading film magazine, reported on her 'bitter outburst'. In the wake of *Silsila*, this signalled a clear attempt by Rekha to continue deploying an association with Bachchan as part of her own star text (see Bose 2006: 305).

23 The director, Yash Chopra, has denied that the casting had been intentional or in response to the frenzied rumours (Dwyer 2002: 120–8).

24 Desai was shooting in Bangalore because he said crowd control in Mumbai would have been 'absolutely impossible' (Haham 2006: 49).

25 Recalling clichéd sequences where the loved ones of a dying character are told by doctors that they can do no more and the only recourse is prayer. On-screen prayers at this point are rewarded with an immediate, miraculous recovery.

26 While Chapter 4 discusses the religious, mythical and epic aspects of stardom, the narrative around Bachchan's injury conflates star text, filmic texts and reality in intriguing ways.

27 See Mishra 2002; Bose 2006.

28 Riding the 'sympathy wave' after Mrs Gandhi's assassination, her son led the party to its most convincing victory in history, with 404 out of 533 seats in the parliament's lower house, the Loksabha.

29 See Virdi 2008 for an interesting analysis of Bachchan's stardom, film text and the Bofors scandal.

30 Astutely, given British libel laws, Bachchan sued *India Abroad* in Britain, where the court found in his favour.

31 Shah Rukh Khan is seen as the heir to Bachchan's 'superstar' status, and continues to produce international hits. The links and contradictions between the star texts of Khan and Bachchan make for interesting study of parallels and contrasts (Singh 2010).

32 See Chopra 2007.

33 The company was relaunched in 2001 as AB Corp, focusing primarily on production, and has since produced several successful films including *Paa* (2009).

34 Mehta notes that the decision came on 10 May 1998, a day before the second round of India's nuclear tests on 11 May 1998. The two decisions seem disparate although may perhaps be linked to the Vajpayee-led government's larger policy towards a muscular nationalist assertion in the international arena.

35 While the exact details of the 'help' provided by Singh, Roy and Anil Ambani are unclear, Bachchan credits the three for their help (Ashraf 2003).

36 See Varma 2007 on the Indian middle class and its post-liberalisation transformation(s).

37 Bachchan debuted in *Yudh* (War) a twenty-episode TV series in July 2014, his first appearance acting on the small screen. The series references Bachchan's 1978 hit *Trishul*, not only in the construction of the industrialist persona but also in the name of his business 'empire'. It is as if *Trishul*'s narrative had continued into the present day, and to the protagonist's twilight years.

38 Journalist Jerry Pinto quoted in Mitra(2012: 572). The 'sermons' were later compiled in a book titled *Soul Curry for You and Me* (2002).

3 A Star Greater than the Industry

1 See Majumdar's discussion on 'efforts to historicize specific cultural contexts for the study of Indian cinema by focussing on stardom' (2009: 11).

2 See Vitali 2008 on the global economic changes that impacted India, setting the conditions that would be ripe for the angry young man.

3 So strong was the impact of food aid on the Indian imaginary that Rajiv Gandhi's 1984 election campaign would refer to it directly to emphasise the economic growth achieved under his mother, Indira Gandhi, since then.

4 See Vanaik 1990.

5 See Vitali 2008. Films from the 1970s to late 1980s – and not only Bachchan's - are consistently preoccupied with the difficulties of balancing the state's view of legality and the necessity of making a living.

6 It must be noted that this is primarily a *savarna*, male, urban and precariously middle-class anxiety, and may be seen as a foreshadowing of the rise of both caste politics in the Hindi heartland in the 1980s and of Hindutva in the 1990s.

7 The film reworks Billy Wilder's *The Apartment* (1960). Its commercial failure suggests that, in addition to aspects of film-making that impacted on its reception, the story found few takers in a primarily non-metropolitan country.

8 See Abraham 1998 for further discussion of the motivations for Pokhran I (India's first nuclear tests in 1974), as well as the way in which post coloniality has informed the national narrative, political stances and policy.

9 Bachchan's violence is also framed in similar moral-not-legal terms, placing his hero safely within the state's narrative of itself. Although no direct link is intended, similar framing is employed by Bachchan's screen persona to legitimise his violence.

10 At the same time, '*Deewar* is a richly polysemic text, skilfully woven for a heterogenous audience, offering a range of possible readings' (Virdi 2008: 225). Virdi is also one of the few scholars who acknowledges, albeit in passing, the 'caste and religious divisions as a subtext buried within class distinctions' (ibid: 15). Barring a few exceptions, scholars' silence on the issue of caste is deafening.

11 Vijay's costume is quite anachronistic for a meeting by a pool and more suited to cooler temperatures (he wears a high-neck jumper under the suit). Yet the signal is subtle: Vijay is a man for climatically and culturally 'cooler' spaces, and not one of the clamouring *hoi polloi* seated around him.

12 In the original version – released in the early 2000s – Gabbar is killed by Thakur in an extended, graphically violent sequence. See Chopra (2000: 148).

13 Prasad, for example, described the film as 'the third high point in the formative phase of the aesthetic of mobilization' (1998: 153).

14 Modernity – in its positive aspects – was long linked to education and a willingness to break away from the 'unjust traditions', including for example, widow remarriage. Such modernity was linked to class as well: see for example *Prem Rog* (Love Is a Disease, 1982).

15 See Prasad 1998.

16 See Raja Rao for homo-erotic readings of Bachchan's films, especially on the relationship of Sher Khan and Vijay in *Zanjeer* (2000).

17 Despite its overt extension of Bachchan's 'angry young man' persona and modern urban setting, the film references Sarat Chandra's classic novel, *Devdas*, and its many filmic versions.

18 The film also reinforces the socially elite status of Bachchan's character: he may 'seem' like a simple mineworker, but in reality hails from a family of naval heroes.

19 The lack of romance in Bachchan films also 'marginalises the female actor' (Mishra 2002: 137), and by extension the female stars, who are relegated to insubstantial glamorous roles, garnering little attention. Female stars who wished to make an impact on their own did so outside of Bachchan films. Also see Virdi 2003. From the mid-1980s however, Bachchan's films attempt to absorb successful female stars from 'parallel cinema' such as Smita Patil in *Shakti* (Power, 1982) and *Namak Halal* (Faithful, 1982) or from south Indian cinemas such as Jayaprada in *Sharaabi* (Drunkard, 1984), and Sridevi in *Aakhree Rasta* (Last Way Out, 1986) and *Khuda Gawah* (God Is Witness, 1992).

20 Poduval notes the casualness with which *Abhimaan* recognises but glosses over corruption and 'black money' as the key to the protagonists' growing wealth (2012).

21 Dasgupta suggests that the star had 'exhausted everything he had to offer' and 'the limits of the hero were known. It was as if the hero had completed the task of finding himself and now it was time for play'(2006: 82).

22 See Vasudevan 2000.

23 Although younger stars including Anil Kapoor, Mithun Chakravarty and increasingly Salman Khan have attempted to reference, even revive the comic element of the 'tough guy', few of the attempts have the conviction of Bachchan. One exception is Shah Rukh Khan's

Main Hoon Na (2004) that pulls off the combination of comedy and 'tough guy' by overtly referencing Bachchan's 1970s persona. A study of 'camp' violence in cinema since the 1970s may yield interesting insights.

24 Film songs have always played a crucial part in the formation of star texts and Bachchan is no exception with his songs circulating independently of the films, first solely as audio texts on radio and cassettes, and then as independent filmic texts on video cassettes, DVDs and television broadcasts (see Mehta 2012).

25 Although Raj Kapoor had drawn on Charlie Chaplin for his screen persona, his characters were also socially, economically and emotionally vulnerable, in contrast to Bachchan's on-screen invulnerability.

26 The sequence also makes subtle but clear points on ethnicity, colonialism and the liminal spaces that must be negotiated by the postcolonial subject. Drawing explicitly on elements of Hollywood's minstrel conventions and explicitly colonial imagery as décor of the gymkhana that Anthony has burst into, the sequence offers a complex polysemic opportunity for considering race, class, and the subaltern.

27 If, as Virdi notes, 'the attrition of the romance sub-plot limited the space for women characters'(2003: 178), Bachchan's ability to subsume the 'item' number marginalised female characters even further.

28 Om Shanti Om (2007) requires a mention. The film actively references late 1970s cinema, although most explicitly evoking Rishi Kapoor's *Karz* (Debt, 1980). The song '*Dard-e-Disco*' explicitly, if parodically, presents Shah Rukh Khan as the object of desire for the spectator. The element of camp in the song actively acknowledges the queering of filmic texts as well as their active consumption.

29 Bhattacharya astutely notes that in the 1980s, Bachchan's 'star aura' is doubled, even tripled, as he plays multiple roles in the same films. She notes that the 'crescendo of the celebration of the vertical hero's potential to present a "larger-than-life" figure of the common man' peaks with *Mahaan* (1982), where he is cast in a triple role, of a father and two sons (2013: 154).

30 See Prasad 2003 for comparison with South Indian film stars whose star texts are not jeopardised by electoral success.

31 While beyond the scope of this study, it is important to consider that Bachchan's most popular films 'almost always coupled him with a range of other masculinities' (Sen 2014: 161) and the 'buddy idiom' was foundational to his stardom (ibid: 143). The failure of films from this period may also be linked to a lack of appropriate on-screen 'buddies' as Bachchan is often paired with younger stars who were themselves attempting to copy and recreate his star persona.

32 Rumours abounded in the late-1970s that the two stars did not work together because of Malini's jealous partner, Dharmendra, although the trio had appeared in the super-hit *Sholay*. The gossip press also attributed the decision to Malini, who apparently preferred to be the top-billed star in her films. The two stars came together for *Naseeb*, *Satte pe Satta* (Seven on Seven, 1982), and *Andha Kanoon* (Blind Justice, 1983) with their rumoured competition providing added piquancy to the films. All three films seemed to avoid highlighting the romantic element, with the last removing it entirely and casting the actress in the role of a police officer looking for vengeance.

33 See Jain 2007.

34 See Srivastava 2014: 22-53 for a discussion of Bachchan's early films in the context of constructions of masculinity and new consumerism in the 1970s.

4 Creation and Re-creation of a Super Star

1 This is not meant to deny Bachchan's overseas appeal but to emphasise that his primary audience is from South Asia.

2 See Chapter 5.

3 See Chakravarty 2013; Sen 2013.

4 See Dyer 1979 for detailed exploration of the ways star images are built over multiple films.

5 Films dating back to Phalke's *Raja Harishchandra* draw both explicitly and implicitly on the two epics. Multiple film, television, and animated productions of narratives based on or drawn from the two texts remain popular. The epics also form an intrinsic part of theatre performance, in folk traditions, contemporary drama, other performance, and fine arts as well as literature.

6 At least part of *Mahābhārata*'s attraction is its moral ambiguity: even though it locates Pandavas as the 'moral' party against the 'immoral' Kauravas, there is little beyond a narrative assertion to support such a claim as the text itself actively undermines simplistic readings of morality, with both sides behaving with varying degrees of duplicity, cruelty, and malice.

7 Echoed by *Deewar*'s crime boss, Davar.

8 A revival of Karna as a storyline and symbol had been churning in post-independence culture well before the film. Nearly twenty years before, Hindi poet Ramdhari Singh Dinkar had published his novel-in-verse, *Rashmirathi* (1954), retelling the epic tale with Karna as the protagonist. Nandy suggests that Karna could symbolically embody the tumult of post-1947 industrialisation and urbanisation. His resurgence in mid-twentieth-century literature and art suggests a particular resonance of his character at this point in India's history.

9 See Nandy 1997 and Kakar 1981, 1983, for further discussion of Karna as the archetype in Bachchan's 1970s cinema.

10 One exception is Tiruvananthapuram's Padmanabhaswamy temple.

11 While beyond the scope of this study, Karna also embodies anxieties around caste privileges (and their loss). The film and Bachchan's Vijay may also be read through this prism.

12 See Mazumdar 2007.

13 Mazumdar notes that Ravi 'represents the state and goes on to cherish the dream of the Emergency' while Vijay critiques and challenges the system and is punished for it (2007: 14).

14 See also Thomas 1995 for discussion of *Deewar* and motherhood.

15 Although a detailed discussion of *rasa* theory is beyond the scope of this study, it provides interesting insights into the structure of Hindi

cinema as well as possibilities for 'genre' classifications.

Of the nine *rasas* – taste or emotions – in art, *virya* (heroic/martial), and *srngāra* (romance/erotic) are the most popular, often providing an overarching structure for a narrative while blending with the remaining *rasas* in ways that reinforce the dominant theme in a work. See Joshi 2004, Schechner 2001 for further discussion on *rasa*.

16 See Raja Rao 2000.

17 See Sen 2014 for detailed discussion of Bachchan's stardom and 'male homosocial bonding'. It may be argued that the 'affective resonance' of characters who are or become like brothers references Arjuna's fraternal bonds in the epic and would be easily recognised by the audience. This 'affective resonance' is also a key aspect of the second epic, Rāmāyana, although it privileges one form of masculinity and its protagonists over others. See Singh 2010, 2008.

18 The song also marks one of Bachchan's early forays into singing for his films. His 'story-song' in *Mr Natwarlal* was officially his first attempt at singing although 'Mere Paas Ao' is more of a recitation than a song.

19 See Singh 2013 for further discussion.

20 See Singh 2013.

21 See Bose 2007.

22 Despite Bachchan's lackadaisical acting and lines delivered in a hoarse voice devoid of all emotion, the film gained him another National Award for Best Actor. Chakravarty for his loud performance of a Tamil street urchin also won the *Filmfare* Best Supporting Actor Award.

23 The epic ends with all heirs of both warring sides destroyed, thus marking complete destruction. A distinctly later amendment reintroduces a note of hope, when an unborn scion is brought 'back to life' and can thus continue the lineage.

24 The period is also marked by a steady decline of the Congress party with 1996 initiating a series of coalition governments, followed by the first government led by then centre-right Bhartiya Janata Party that had led the Ayodhya campaign earlier in the decade.

25 See Singh 2008, 2010.

26 As has often been the case with Bachchan's long career, his on-screen persona is reinforced by multiple texts. In 2013, the actor provided the voice-over for Bhishma in an animated version of the *Mahābhārata*.

27 The name means one who has taken a terrible oath, a reference to his vow of celibacy.

28 Many of the *Ramlilas* – or annual ritual re-enactments of the *Rāmāyana*– feature an incident when Ravana learns that his slayer has been born and travels to Ayodhya to kill the infant Rama. However on seeing the child at play, he changes his mind and spares him, despite knowing his own fate. The anecdote is popularly evoked as the power of the Rama as a 'benevolent' deity who can 'melt hearts'.

29 Bachchan's roles after *Mohabbatein* suggest intriguing ways of extending Sen's argument of homosocial bonding as a continuing aspect of his stardom (2014).

30 See Mishra (2002: 154); Mitra (2012: 569–72).

31 See Chakravarty 1993; Mazumdar 2000; Mishra 2002; Prasad 1998.

32 See Bhattacharya 2013 for a detailed discussion of how the camera use in Bachchan's films echoed his rising star status and reaffirmed his persona (2013).

33 According to the 2011 census, only 4 percent of the country's population is above sixty-four years of age, while 81 percent is under the age of 45: http://censusindia.gov.in/Census_And_You/age_structure_and_marital_status.aspx.

34 Indeed, the star's reinvented avatar and the changes in the film industry have helped bridge the gap between 'commercial' and 'parallel' or art cinema, with filmmakers like Nihalani or Jha who would or could not have worked with Bachchan in the 1970s and 1980s making films with the star in post-2000 years.

35 The film is also intriguing as many of the techniques employed by the activists were seen in real life in the 2014 general elections.

36 The 2012 protests against a gang-rape and murder of a young woman in a bus in New Delhi broke out nation-wide and continued for months until a new rape law was rushed through parliament. The protests were brutally countered, especially in Delhi, with water cannons and tear gas. They were not only the largest protests to date against violence against women anywhere in the world, but also the first public political mass action of a very youthful generation in India.

5 Impact on Contemporary Cultural Production

1 See Dwyer 2000.
2 See Chapter 4.
3 Chopra notes that Khan was part of a generation that modelled their haircuts on Bachchan's and the younger star 'knew he had attained stardom when hairstylists told him that clients were asking for the Shah Rukh Khan cut' (2007: 44).
4 The film's framing of Hindu right-wing violence as individualised mental illness rather than a political phenomenon provides a cover for some of its troubling representations of minorities: Rauf Lala's religious affiliation and exuberant participation in ritual demonise one minority, while the replacement of Mary by Kaali renders another invisible.
5 In an apparent rebuttal of criticisms that in contrast to Hollywood, Hindi cinema lacks 'realism', the film also spoofs *The Matrix* (1999) for comic effect.
6 The director referenced the 1970s epic cinema more overtly in *Om Shanti Om* (2007), a homage to *Karz* (Debt 1980). The film also refers to Bachchan's oeuvre and includes a *Naseeb*-like song sequence set at a 'star' party.
7 The film makes it clear that Faizal recognises the adult Mohsina as the little girl begging to be let in to see films that he had seen years before, replicating the 'romance' trope of Bachchan's films where a childhood bond is rediscovered in adulthood.

8 Srivastava makes a compelling case for Bachchan's impact on the construction of masculinity and an early consumerist agenda. This shift from the delayed gratification of the 'Five Year Plan' hero to the impatient aggression of the neo-liberal aspirant, insisting that he get his due immediately is also one that can partially explain why the star could reinvent himself so effectively for the post-liberalisation era in the 1990s.

9 The appearance of stars as themselves in films is a long-standing convention, used generally to reinforce filmic 'realism' and reassert the importance of the star, or filmmaker. In Desai's *Naseeb*, a bevy of stars attend the 'golden jubilee' celebration for the director's earlier hit *Dharam-Veer* (1977). Screen appearances of the stars 'being themselves' and especially at glamorous parties also function to assert their glamour and mystique: the reel-life version of their ostensibly 'real' lives reaffirming audience's assumptions of fabulously luxurious lifestyles.

10 In *Ramji Londonwale,* the star humorously bemoans the ability of fans to see him 'anytime they like' simply by buying a ticket while he must seek them out individually.

11 Murabba in north India is generally a sweet fruit preserve, with the most popular version using whole gooseberries.

12 See Singh 2008, 2010 for discussions of *darśana* in the construction of star texts.

13 The term also applies to the six 'orthodox' philosophical traditions in India with the word used for seeing cosmic truths. As Eck points out: 'There are many such *darśana*, many "points of view", or "perspectives" on the truth ... Any 'point of view' implicitly assumes that another point of view is possible' (Eck 1996: 25).

14 Coorlawala critiques the application of Laura Mulvey's scopophilia as a default critical model for viewership, suggesting that it is not the primary mechanism activated by cinema for the Indian viewer.

15 See Booth 2000 for further discussion on *darśana* and the cultural codes that inform meanings made from its activation.

16 It is interesting to note the ways Hindi cinema engages with and extends the Indic philosophical concept of material reality as *maya* or illusion.

17 Mishra lists the song sequences as one of the unique features of stardom in Indian cinema (2002).
18 See Mehta 2012 for the role of song compilation in film consumption.

6 Conclusion

1 See Singh 2013.
2 Curiously this seems to be especially the case for formidable male stars. Female stars including Aishwarya Rai Bachchan have attempted to 'cross over' to Western cinema. However, so far all cross-overs have only had limited success, regardless of gender.
3 The panel was part of the twenty-fifth anniversary programming https://www.youtube.com/watch?v=3pkJ5tUXgTs.
4 Accessed: https://www.youtube.com/watch?v=amtgOllXRc4.
5 *Piku* uses the name of Bachchan's character from *Anand* (1971). Sircar notes of his character that 'he's an older Babumoshai'.' Accessed here: http://www.pinkvilla.com/entertainmenttags/amitabh-bachchan/how-big-b-s-piku-character-connected-his-1971-hit-anand.
6 See http://www.hollywoodreporter.com/news/graphic-india-disney-channel-india-802730.
7 In an interview with Nayandeep Rakshit for DNA. Accessed here: http://www.dnaindia.com/entertainment/interview-i-don-t-search-for-my-daughter-in-deepika-amitabh-bachchan-on-piku-2084944.

REFERENCES

Abraham, Itty. *The Making of the Indian Atomic Bomb: Science, Secrecy and the Postcolonial State*. New York: Zed Books, 1998.

Aftab, Kaleem. "Brown: The New Black! Bollywood in Britain." In *Critical Quarterly*, Vol. 44, No. 3, 2002, pp. 88–98.

Anonymous: "Bollywood Star Tops the Poll." In BBC News, 1 July 1999. Available online at: http://news.bbc.co.uk/1/hi/entertainment/381017.stm.

Ashraf, Firdaus Syed. "There Was a Sword Hanging Over My Head: Amitabh." In *Rediff*, October 12, 2003. Accessed here: http://www.rediff.com/movies/2003/oct/11ab.htm.

Babb, Lawrence A. and Wadley, Susan (eds). *Media and the Transformation of Religion in South Asia*. Philadelphia: University Pennsylvania Press, 1995.

Babb, Lawrence, A. *Redemptive Encounters: Three Modern Styles in the Hindu Tradition*. Berkeley: University of California Press, 1987.

____________. "Glancing: Visual Interaction in Hinduism." In *Journal of Anthropological Research*, Vol. 37, No. 4, 1981, pp. 387–401.

Bachchan, Amitabh. *Soul Curry for You and Me*. Mumbai: Popular Books, 2002.

Banerjea, Koushik. ""Fight Club": Aesthetics, Hybridisation and the Construction of Rogue Masculinities in *Sholay* and *Deewar*." In Kaur, Raminder and Sinha, Ajay J. (ed), *Bollyworld: Popular Indian Cinema Through a Transnational Lens*. New Delhi: Sage Publications Ltd, 2005, pp. 163–85.

Becker, Christine. *It's the Pictures that Got Smaller: Hollywood Film Stars on 1950s Television*. Middleton: Wesleyan University Press, 2008.

Beltran, Mary, Creekmur, Cory, Gopal, Sangita and Raphael, Raphael. "A Panel Discussion on Transnational Stardom." In Meeuf, Russell and Raphael, Raphael (eds), *Transnational Stardom: International Celebrity in Film and Popular Culture (Global Film)*. New York: Palgrave Macmillan, 2013 (N.pag. Kindle file).

Bennett, Peter. "In Nanda Baba's House. The Devotional Experience in Pushti Marg Temples." In Lynch, Owen M. (ed), *Divine Passions: The Social Construction of Emotion in India*. Berkeley: University of California Press, 1990, pp. 189–96.

Bhatia, Sidharth. *Amar, Akbar, Anthony: Masala, Madness, Manmohan Desai*. New Delhi: Harper Collins India, 2013.

Bhattacharjea, Ajit. *Unfinished Revolution: A Political Biography of Jayaprakash Narayan*. New Delhi: Rupa Publications, 2004.

Bhattacharya, Nandini. *Hindi Cinema: Repeating the Subject*. Abingdon, Oxon: Routledge, 2013.

Bhattacharya Mehta, Rini and Pandharipande, Rajeshwari V. *Bollywood and Globalization: Indian Popular Cinema, Nation and the Diaspora*. London: Anthem Press, 2011.

Bhaumik, Saba Naqvi. "Politics of Indian War Films." In *South Asian Journal*, Vol. 10, 2005, pp. 85–93.

Booth, Gregory D. "Traditional Content and Narrative Structure in the Hindi Commercial Cinema." In *Asian Folklore Studies*, Vol. 54, No. 2, 1995, pp. 169–90.

____________. "Religion, Gossip, Narrative Conventions and the Construction of Meaning in Hindi Film Songs." In *Popular Music*, Vol. 19, No. 2, 2000, pp. 125–45.

Bordwell, David. "Historical Poetics of Cinema." In Palmer, Barton (ed), *The Cinematic Text: Methods and Approaches*. Atlanta: Georgia State University Press, 1988.

Bose, Mihir. *Bollywood: A History*. New Delhi: Roli Books, 2007.

Campbell, Joseph. *The Hero With a Thousand Faces (Collected Works)*. Novaro: New World Library, 2008 (original 1949) .

Chandra, Pradeep. *AB The Legend: A Photographer's Tribute*. New Delhi: Rupa, 2006.

Chakravarty, Sumita S. "Con-figurations: The Body as World in Bollywood Stardom." In Sen, Meheli and Basu, Anustup (eds), *Figurations in Indian Film*. London: Palgrave Macmillan, 2013, pp. 179–204.

____________. *National Identity in Indian Popular Cinema, 1947–1987*. Austin: University of Texas Press, 1993.

Chopra, Anupama. *King of Bollywood: Shah Rukh Khan and the Seductive World of Indian Cinema*. New York: Warner Books, 2007.

Chute, David. "The Rise and Fall and Rebirth of Bollywood Superstar Amitabh Bachchan." In *Film Comment*, Vol. 41, No. 2, 2005. Accessed here: http://www.filmcomment.com/article/the-rise-and-fall-and-rebirth-of-bollywood-superstar-amitabh-bachchan.

Coorlawala, Uttara Asha. "It Matters for Whom You Dance: Audience Participation in Rasa Theory." In Susan Kattwinkel (ed), *Audience Participation: Essays on Inclusion in Performance*. Westport: Praeger Publishers, 2003.

____________. "Darshan and Abhinaya: An Alternative to the Male Gaze." In *Dance Research Journal*, Vol. 28, No. 1, Spring 1996, pp. 19–27.

Creekmur, Corey K. "Bombay Boys: Dissolving the Male Child in Popular Hindi Cinema." In *Where the Boys Are: Cinemas of Boyhood*, ed. Murray Pomerance and Frances Gateward. Detroit: Wayne State University Press, 2004, pp. 350–76.

Dasgupta, Susmita. *Amitabh: The Making of a Superstar*. Penguin Books, 2006.

____________. "Sarkar: Re-presenting Amitabh Bachchan." In *Economic and Political Weekly*, Vol. 40, No. 38, Sept 17–23, 2005, pp. 4105–08.

Dawson, Ashley. "Bollywood Flashback: Hindi Film Music and the Negotiation of Identity among British-Asian Youths." In *South Asian Popular Culture*, Vol. 3, No. 2, 2005, pp. 161–76.

Derné, Steve. *Movies, Masculinity, and Modernity: An Ethnography of Men's Filmgoing in India*. Westport: Greenwood Press, 2000.

Desai, Jigna. *Beyond Bollywood: The Cultural Politics of South Asian Diasporic Film*. New York: Routledge, 2004.

Desai, Jigna and Dudrah, Rajinder. *The Essential Bollywood*. London: The Open University Press, 2008.

Dickey, Sara. "The Politics of Adulation: Cinema and the Production of Politicians in South India." In *The Journal of Asian Studies*, Vol. 52, No. 2, May 1993, pp. 340–72.

Dinkar, Ramdhari Singh. *Rashmirathi*. Allahabad: Lokbharti Prakashan, 1954.

Dudrah, Rajinder. *Bollywood: Sociology Goes to the Movies*. New Delhi: Sage Publications India Pvt. Ltd, 2006.

Dudrah, Rajinder and Rai, Amit. "The Haptic Codes of Bollywood Cinema in New York City." In *New Cinemas: Journal of Contemporary Film,* Vol. 3, No. 3, 2005, pp. 143–58.

Dwyer, Rachel and Patel, D. *Cinema India: The Visual Culture of Hindi Film*, New Brunswick: Rutgers University Press, 2002.

Dwyer, Rachel. "The Hindi Romantic Cinema: Yash Chopra's *Kabhie Kabhie* and *Silsila*." In *South Asia: Journal of South Asian Studies*, Vol. 21, No. 1, 1998, pp. 181–212.

____________. *All You Want is Money, All You Need is Love: Sexuality and Romance in Modern India*. London and New York: Cassell, 2000.

____________. "I Love You When You're Angry': Amitabh Bachchan, Emotion and the Star in the Hindi Film." In Bandhauer, Andrea and Royer, Michelle (eds), *Stars in World Cinema: Screen Icons and Star Systems Across Cultures*. London: IB Tauris, 2015, pp. 13–23.

Dyer, Richard. *Heavenly Bodies: Film Stars and Society*. London: British Film Institute, 1986.

____________. *Stars*. London: British Film Institute, 1979.

____________. *White*. London: Routledge, 1997.

____________. *The Matter of Images: Essays of Representations*. London: Routledge, 1993.

Eck, Diana. *Darsan: Seeing the Divine Image in India*. Chambersburg: Anima Books, 1981.

Elison, William, Novetzke, Christian Lee and Rotman, Andy. *Amar Akbar Anthony: Bollywood, Brotherhood and the Nation.* Cambridge: Harvard University Press, 2016.

Ellis, John. *Visible Functions: Cinema, Television, Video.* London: Routledge, 1992 (1982).

Gaffney, John and Holmes, Diana (eds). *Stardom in Postwar France.* NewYork: Berghahn Books, 2007.

____________. "Stardom in Theory and Context." In Gaffney, John and Holmes, Diana (eds), *Stardom in Postwar France.* New York: Berghahn Books, 2007 pp. 7–25.

Gandhy, Behroze and Thomas, Rosie. "Three Indian Stars." In Gledhill, Christine (ed), *Stardom: Industry of Desire.* London: Routledge, 1991, pp. 111–35.

Garwood, Ian. "The Songless Bollywood Film." In *South Asian Popular Culture,* Vol. 4, No. 2, 2006, pp. 169–83.

Ghosh, Bishnupriya. "Sensate Outlaws: The Recursive Social Bandit in Indian Popular Cultures." In Sen, Meheli and Basu, Anustup (eds), *Figurations in Indian Film.* London: Palgrave Macmillan, 2013, pp. 21–43.

____________. *Global Icons: Apertures to the Popular.* Durham: Duke University Press, 2011, pp. 169–70.

Gokulsing, Moti, K and Dissanayake, Wimal. *From Aan to Lagaan and Beyond: A Guide to the Study of Indian Cinema.* Stoke on Trent: Trentham Books, 2012.

Gopal, Sangita and Moorti, Sujata (ed), *Global Bollywood: Travels of Hindi Song and Dance.* Minneapolis: University of Minnesota Press, 2008.

Gopinath, Gayatri. "Queering Bollywood: Alternative Sexualities in Popular Indian Cinema." In Grossman, Andrew (ed), *Queer Asian Cinema: Shadows in the Shade.* New York: Harrington Park Press, 2000, pp. 283–99.

Govil, Nitin. "Bollywood and the Frictions of Global Mobility." In Thussu, Daya (ed), *Global Media Bazaar: Global Flow and Contra-Flow.* New York: Routledge, 2007, pp. 76–88.

Haham, Connie. *Enchantment of the Mind: Manmohan Desai's Films*. New Delhi: Roli Books, 2005.

Hansen, Kathryn. "Language, Community and the Theatrical Public: Linguistic Pluralism and Change in the Nineteenth-Century Parsi Theatre." In Blackburn, Stuart and Dalmia, Vasudha (eds), *India's Literary History: Essays on the Nineteenth Century*. New Delhi: Permanent Black, 2004, pp. 60–86.

____________. "The *Inder sabha* Phenomenon: Public Theatre and Consumption in Greater India (1853–1956)." In Rachel Dwyer and Christopher Pinney (eds), *Pleasure and the Nation: The Politics and Consumption of Popular Culture in India*. New Delhi: Oxford University Press, 2000.

____________. *Grounds for Play: The Nautanki Theatre in North India*. Berkeley: University of California Press, 1992.

Hariharan, K. "Revisiting Sholay a.k.a Flames of the Sun." In *Asian Cinema,* Vol. 10, No. 2, March 1999, pp. 151–54.

Henniker, Charlie. "Pink Rupees or Gay Icons? Accounting for the Camp Appropriation of Male Bollywood Stars." In Meeuf, Russell and Raphael, Raphael (eds). *Transnational Stardom: International Celebrity in Film and Popular Culture (Global Film)*. New York: Palgrave Macmillan, 2013, pp. 207–28.

Hines, Jessica. *Looking for The Big B: Bollywood, Bachchan and Me*. London: Bloomsbury, 2007.

Jain, Kajri. *Gods in the Bazaar: The Economies of Indian Calendar Art*. Durham: Duke University Press, 2007.

Jain, Varsha, Roy, Subhadip, Daswani, Arzoo and Sudha, Mari. "How Celebrities are Used in Indian Television Commercials." In *Vikalpa: The Journal for Decisionmakers*, Vol. 35, No. 4, October–December 2010, pp. 45–52.

Jeyathurai, Dashini. "Rethinking the Circuits of Male Desire Across Multiple Dostanas." In Dasgupta, Rohit K and Gokulsing Moti K. (eds), *Masculinity and Its Challenges in India: Essays on Changing Perceptions*. Jefferson: McFarland & Co Inc., 2013, pp. 227–40.

Jha, Priya. "Lyrical Nationalism: Gender, Friendship, and Excess in 1970s Hindi Cinema." In *The Velvet Light Trap*, Vol. 51, Spring 2003, pp. 43–53.

Jones, Matthew. "Bollywood, *Rasa*, and Indian Cinema: Misconceptions, Meanings and *Millionnaire*." In *Visual Anthropology*, Vol. 23, No. 1, 2009, pp. 33–43.

Joshi, Sam. "How to Watch a Hindi Film, the Example of *Kuch Kuch Hota Hai*." In *Education About Asia*, Vol. 9, No. 1, 2004, pp. 22–25.

Kakar, Sudhir. "The Cinema as Collective Fantasy." In Aruna Vasudev and Philippe Lenglet (eds), *Indian Cinema Superbazaar*. New Delhi: Vikas Publishing House, 1983, pp. 89–97.

____________. "The Ties that Bind: Family Relationships in the Mythology of Hindi Cinema." In *India International Quarterly*, Vol. 8, No. 1, 1981, pp. 11–22.

Kasbekar, Asha. "Hidden Pleasures: Negotiating the Myth of the Female Ideal in Popular Hindi Cinema." In Rachel Dwyer and Christopher Pinney (eds), *Pleasure and the Nation: Politics and Consumption of Public Culture in India*. New Delhi: Oxford University Press, 2000, pp. 286–308.

Kaur, Raminder and Sinha, Ajay J (eds). *Bollyworld: Popular Indian Cinema Through a Transnational Lens*. New Delhi: Sage Publications Ltd, 2005.

Kavi, Ashok Row. "The Changing Image of the Hero in Hindi Films." In Grossman, Andrew (ed), *Queer Asian Cinema: Shadows in the Shade*. New York: Harrington Park Press, 2000, pp. 307–13.

Kavoori, Anandam and Punathambekar, Aswin. *Global Bollywood*. New York: New York University Press, 2008.

Kazmi, Fareeduddin. "How Angry is the Angry Young Man? Rebellion in Conventional Hindi Films." In Nandy, Ashis (ed), *The Secret Politics of Our Desires: Innocence, Culpability and Indian Popular Cinema*. New Delhi: Oxford University Press, 1998a, pp. 134–56.

Kazmi, Nikhat. *The Dream Merchants of Bollywood*. New Delhi: UBS Publishers, 1998b.

____________. *Ire in the Soul: Bollywood's Angry Years*. New Delhi: Harper Collins, 1996.

Kesavan, Mukul. "An Undergraduate History of Hindi Cinema." In Verghese, B.G. (ed), *Tomorrow's India, Another Tryst with Destiny*. New Delhi: Penguin Books India, 2006, pp. 320–29.

Kreuger, Oliver. "It's All about Loving Your Parents': The Reflection of Tradition, Modernity and Rituals in Popular Indian Movies." In *Marburg Journal of Religion*, Vol. 9, No. 1, September 2004. Accessed here: http://archiv.ub.uni-marburg.de/mjr/art_krueger_2004.html.

Kripalani, Coonoor. "Trendsetting and Product Placement in Bollywood Film: Consumerism Through Consumption." In *New Cinemas: Journal of Contemporary Film*, Vol. 4, No. 3, February 2007, pp. 197–215.

Kumar, Shanti. "Innovation, Imitation, and Hybridity in Indian Television." In Edgerton, Gary R. and Rose, Brian G. (eds), *Thinking Outside the Box: A Contemporary Television Genre Reader*. Lexington: University of Kentucky Press, 2005, pp. 314–35.

____________. "Who Wants to be a Crorepati?: Global Television and Local Genres in India." Accessed here: http://flowtv.org/2005/02/who-wants-to-be-a-crorepati-global-television-and-local-genres-in-india/.

Lal, Vinay. *Deewar: The Footpath, The City and the Angry Young Man*. New Delhi: Harper Collins Publishers India, 2011.

Larkin, Brian. "Bandiri Music, Globalisation and Urban Experience in Nigeria." In Kaur, Raminder and Sinha, Ajay J (eds), *Bollyworld: Popular Indian Cinema Through a Transnational Lens*. New Delhi: Sage Publications, 2005, pp. 284–308.

____________. "Itineraries of Indian Cinema: African Videos, Bollywood, and Global Media." In *Multiculturalism, Postcoloniality and Transnational Media*." Ella Shohat and Robert Stam (eds), New Brunswick: Rutgers University Press, 2003, pp. 170–92.

____________. "Indian Films and Nigerian Lovers: Media and the Creation of Parallel Modernities." In *Africa: Journal of the International African Institute*, Vol. 67, No. 3, 1997, pp. 406–40.

Liang, Lawrence. "Cinematic Citizenship and the Illegal City." In *Inter-Asia Cultural Studies*, Vol. 6, No. 3, 2005, pp. 366–85.

Lutgendorf, Philip. "A Superhit Goddess: *Jai Santoshi Maa* and Caste Hierarchy in Indian Films." In *Manushi*, Vol. 131, No. 10–16 (July–August 2002), pp. 24–37. Accessed here: http://www.columbia.edu/itc/mealac/pritchett/00generallinks/lutgendorf_santoshi/txt_lutgendorf_santoshi.html.

Majumdar, Neepa. *Wanted Cultured Ladies Only: Female Stardom and Cinema in India*, 1930s–1950s. Champaign: University of Illinois Press, 2009.

Mazumdar, Ranjani. "Film Stardom after Liveness." In *Continuum: Journal of Media & Cultural Studies*, Vol. 26, No. 2, 2012, pp. 833–44.

____________. "The Man Who Was Seen Too Much: Amitabh Bachchan on Film Posters." In *Tasveer Ghar: A Digital Network of South Asian Popular Visual Culture*, Coordinated by Sumathy Ramaswamy, Christiane Brossius, Manishita Das and Yuousuf Sayeed, 2010. Accessed here: http://tasveergharindia.net/cmsdesk/essay/106/index.html.

____________. *Bombay Cinema: An Archive of the City*. Minneapolis: University of Minnesota Press, 2007.

____________. "From Subjectification to Schizophrenia: The 'Angry Young Man' and the 'Psychotic' Hero of Bombay Cinema." In Ravi. S. Vasudevan (ed), *Making Meaning in Indian Cinema*. New Delhi: Oxford University Press, 2000, pp. 238–64.

Mazzarella, William. *Shoveling Smoke: Advertising and Globalization in Contemporary India*. Durham: Duke University Press, 2003.

Mehta, Monika. "DVD Compilations of Hindi Film Songs: (Re-)shuffling Sound, Stardom, and Cinephilia." In *South Asian Popular Culture*, Vol. 10, No. 3, 2012, pp. 237–48.

____________. "Globalizing Bombay Cinema: Reproducing the Indian State and Family." In *Cultural Dynamics*, Vol. 17, No. 2, 2016, pp. 135–54.

Mehta, Suketu. "Welcome to Bollywood." In *National Geographic*. 2005. Accessed here: http://ngm.nationalgeographic.com/ngm/0502/feature3/index.html.

Mellor, Noha, Rinnawi, Khalil, Dajani, Nabil, and Ayish Muhammad. *Arab Media: Globalization and Emerging Media Industries*. Cambridge: Polity Press, 2011.

Mishra, Vijay. *Bollywood Cinema: Temples of Desire*. London, New York: Routledge, 2002.

____________. "Filmic Narrative: Text and Transformation in Bombay Cinema." In *Continuum: Journal of Media and Cultural Studies*, Vol. 2, No. 1, 1998, pp. 9–43.

Mishra, Vijay, Jeffrey, Peter and Shoesmith, Brian. "The Actor as Parallel Text in Bombay Cinema." In *Quarterly Review of Film and Video*, Vol. 1, No. 3, 1989, pp. 49–67.

Mitra, Sreya. "From Heroine to 'Brand Shilpa': Reality Television, Transnational Cultural Economies, and the Remaking of the Bollywood Star." In Meeuf, Russell and Raphael, Raphael (eds), *Transnational Stardom: International Celebrity in Film and Popular Culture (Global Film)*. New York: Palgrave Macmillan, 2013, pp. 187–206.

____________. "'The Show of the Millennium': Screening the Big Money Quiz Show and the Bollywood Superstar." In *South Asian History and Culture*, Vol. 3, No. 4, 2012, pp. 566–82.

Mohamed, Khalid. "AB Baby's Day Out." Undated interview from late 1990s. 1997. Accessed here: http://www.sugandh.com/seema/amitabhji/khalid.html.

Morcom, Anna. *Hindi Film Songs and the Cinema* (SOAS Musicology Series). Aldershot: Ashgate, 2007.

Moseley, R. *Fashioning Film Stars?: Dress, Culture, Identity*. London: British Film Institute, 2005.

Murray, Susan. *Hitch Your Antenna to the Stars: Early Television and Broadcast Stardom*. New York: Routledge, 2005.

Nandy, Ashis. (ed). *The Secret Politics of Our Desires: Innocence, Culpability and Indian Popular Cinema*. New Delhi: Oxford University Press, 1998.

Oza, Rupal. *The Making of Neo-Liberal India: Nationalism, Gender and the Paradoxes of Globalization*. New York: Routledge, 2012.

Pal, Colin. *Shooting Stars*. Mumbai: A Screen World Publication. 2004.

Pauwels, Heidi R.M (ed). *Indian Literature and Popular Cinema*. New York: Routledge, 2007.

Poduval, Satish. "The Affable Young Man: Civility, Desire and the Making of a Middle-Class Cinema in the 1970s." In *South Asian Popular Culture*, Vol. 10, No. 1, 2012, pp. 37–50.

____________. "Obscure Subjects of Desire: Gender, Conjugality, and the Remaking of Class in 1970s Hindi Cinema." http://www.cla.temple.edu/chat/india/documents/Poduval.pdf.

Prasad, M. Madhava. *Ideology of the Hindi Film: A Historical Construction.* New Delhi: Oxford University Press, 1998.

____________. "Reigning Stars: The Political Career of South Indian Cinema." In Fischer, Lucy and Landy, Marcia (eds), *Stars: The Film Reader*. New York: Routledge, 2004, pp. 97–114.

Punathambekar, Aswin. "Bollywood in the Indian-American diaspora: Mediating a Transitive Logic of Cultural Citizenship." In *International Journal of Cultural Studies*, Vol. 8, No. 2, 2005, pp. 151–73.

____________. "From Bihar to Manhattan: Bollywood and the Transnational Indian Family" Accessed here: http://www-personal.umich.edu/~aswinp/Transnational-family.pdf.

Rabine, L.W., and S. Kaiser. "Sewing Machines and Dream Machines in Los Angeles and San Francisco." In C. Breward and D. Gilbert (eds), *Fashion's World Cities*. Oxford: Berg, 2006, pp. 235–50.

Raheja, Dinesh and Kothari, Jitendra. *The 100 Stars of Indian Cinema* (with introduction by Amitabh Bachchan). Bombay: India Book House Publishers, 1996.

Raj, Ashok. *Hero: Amitabh Bachchan to the Khans and Beyond*. London: Hay House, 2010.

Raja Rao, R. "Memories Piece the Heart: Homoeroticism, Bollywood-Style." In *Journal of Homosexuality*, 39 (3–4), 2000, pp. 299–306.

Rajadhyaksha, Ashish. "An Aesthetic for Film Sound in India." Accessed here: http://www.jmionline.org/articles/2007/An_Aesthetic_for_Fil.pdf.

Rajadhyaksha, Ashish and Willemen, Paul (eds). *Encyclopedia of Indian Cinema*. London: Routledge, 1994.

Roy, Subhadip. "An Exploratory Study in Celebrity Endorsements." In *Journal of Creative Communications*, Vol. 1, No. 2, July 2006, pp. 139–53.

Samant, Sapna. "Appropriating Bollywood Cinema: Why the Western World Gets Bollywood so Wrong." In *Metro Magazine: Media & Education Magazine*, Vol. 145, 2005, pp. 82–85.

Schechner, Richard. "Rasaesthetics." In *TDR: The Drama Review*, Vol. 45, No. 3, Autumn 2001, pp. 27–50.

____________. *Between Theatre and Anthropology*. Philadelphia: University of Pennsylvania Press, 1985.

Sen, Krishna. "The Language of Violence in Indonesian Cinema." In *New Cinemas: Journal of Contemporary Film*, Vol. 8, No. 3, January 2011, pp. 202–12.

Sen, Meheli. "From *Dostana* to Bromance: Buddies in Indian Commercial Cinema Reconsidered." In DeAngelis, Michael (ed), *Reading the Bromance: Homosocial Relationships in Film and Television.* Detroit: Wayne State University Press, 2014, pp. 139–64.

____________. "Introduction." In Sen, Meheli and Basu, Anustup (eds), *Figurations in Indian Film*. London: Palgrave Macmillan, 2013, pp. 1–20.

____________. "'It's All About Loving Your Parents': Liberalization, Hindutva, and Bollywood's New Fathers." In Bhattacharya Mehta, Rini and Pandharipande, Rajeshwari V. (eds), *Bollywood and Globalization: Indian Popular Cinema, Nation and the Diaspora.* London: Anthem Press, 2011, pp. 145–68.

Shapiro Anjaria, Jonathan. *Unruly Streets: Everyday Practices and Promises of Globality in Mumbai.* Ann Arbor: Proquest, UMI Dissertation Publishing, 2011, pp. 90–91.

Sharma, Ashwani. "Blood, Sweat and Tears: Amitabh Bachchan, Urban Demi-God." In Pat Kirkham and Janet Thumim (eds), *You Tarzan: Masculinity, Movies and Men.* New York: St. Martin's Press, 1993, pp. 167–80.

Shingler, Martin. *Star Studies: A Critical Guide.* London: BFI/Palgrave Macmillan, 2012.

Singh, Sunny. "Towards an Inclusive, Fluid Construction of Gender and Sexual in Commercial Indian Cinema(s)." In Diana Dimitrova (ed.), *The Other in South Asian Religion, Literature and Film: Perspectives on Otherism and Otherness.* New York: Routledge, 2013, pp. 138–60.

____________. "From Kurukshetra to Ramarajya: A Comparative Analysis of the Star Personas of Amitabh Bachchan and Shah Rukh Khan. In Dimitrova, Diana (ed), *Religion in Literature and Film in South Asia.* New York: Palgrave Macmillan, 2010, pp. 213–22.

____________. 2008. "The Road to Rāmarājya: Analysing Shah Rukh Khan's Parallel Text in Commercial Hindi Cinema." In *BELLS* Vol. 17, Autumn 2008.

Somaaya, Bhawana. *Amitabh Bachchan, the Legend.* New Delhi: Macmillan India Ltd, 1999.

Srivastava, Sanjay. "Sane Sex," the Five Year Plan Hero and Men on Footpaths and in Gated Communities: On the Cultures of Twentieth Century Masculinity." In Dasgupta, Rohit K and Gokulsing Moti K. (eds), *Masculinity and Its Challenges in India: Essays on Changing Perceptions.* Jefferson: McFarland & Co Inc., 2013, pp. 27–53.

Stephens Duncan, Rebecca. "Reading Slumdog Millionaire across Cultures." In *The Journal of Commonwealth Literature,* Vol. 46, No. 2, 2011, pp. 311–26.

Tharoor, Shashi. *India: From Midnight to the Millennium.* New York: Harper Collins, 1998.

Thomas, Rosie. "Melodrama and the Negotiation of Morality in Mainstream Hindi Film." In Breckenridge, Carol A. (ed), *Consuming Modernity: Public Culture in a South Asian World.* Minneapolis: University of Minnesota Press, 1995, pp. 157–82.

____________. "Sanctity and Scandal: The Mythologization of Mother India." In *Quarterly Review of Film & Video,* Vol. 11, 1989, pp. 11–30.

Thussu, Daya Kishan. "Infotainment Inc.: The Ascent of a Global Ideology." In Papathanassopoulos, Stylianos (ed), *Media Perspectives for the 21st Century.* NY: Routledge, 2011, pp. 68–82.

Tyrell, Heather. "Bollywood vs Hollywood: Battle of the Dream Factories." In Allen, Tim and Skelton, Tracey (eds), *Culture and Global Change.* London: Routledge, 1999, pp. 260–73.

Vachani, Lalit. "Bachchan-alias: The Many Faces of a Film Icon." In Christiane Brosius and Melissa Butcher (eds) *Image Journeys: Audio-Visual Media & Cultural Change in India.* New Delhi: Sage Publications India Pvt Ltd, 1999, pp. 199–230.

Vanaik, Achin. *The Painful Transition: Bourgeois Democracy in India.* London and New York: Verso, 1990.

Varia, Kush. *Bollywood: Gods, Glamour, and Gossip.* New York: A Wallflower Press Book, Columbia University Press, 2012.

Varma, Pavan. *The Great Indian Middle Class.* New Delhi: Penguin Books India, 2007.

Vasudevan, Ravi: "The Exhilaration of Dread: Genre, Narrative Form and Film Style in Contemporary Urban Action Films.' In Kaarsholm, Preben (ed), *City Flicks: Indian Cinema and the Urban Experience*. London: Seagull Books, 2007, pp. 219–32.

____________. "The Politics of Cultural Address in a "Transitional" Cinema: A Case Study of Popular Indian Cinema." In Gledhill, Christine and Williams, Linda (eds), *Reinventing Film Studies*. London: Bloomsbury Academic, 2000a, pp. 130–64.

____________. "Shifting Codes, Dissolving Identities: The Hindi Social Film of the 1950s as Popular Culture." In Vasudevan, R. (ed), *Making Meaning in Indian Cinema*. New Delhi: Oxford University Press, 2000b, pp. 99–121.

Virdi, Jyotika. "*Deewar*/Wall (1975): Fact, Fiction, and the Making of a Superstar." In Kavoori, Anandam and Punathambekar, Aswin (eds), *Global Bollywood*. New York: New York University Press, 2008, pp. 223–39.

____________. *The Cinematic Imagination: Indian Popular Films as Social History*. New Brunswick: Rutgers University Press, 2003.

____________. "Deewar: The 'Fiction' of Film and 'Fact' of Politics.' In *Jump Cut: A Review of Contemporary Media*, Vol. 38, June 1993, pp. 26–32.

Visvanathan, Shiv. "The Crorepati Narratives." In *Economic and Political Weekly*, Vol. 35, No. 35/36, August 26–September 8, 2000. Accessed here: http://www.epw.in/journal/2000/35-36/commentary/crorepati-narratives.html.

Vitali, Valentina. *Hindi Action Cinema: Industries, Narratives, Bodies*. Bloomington and Indianapolis: Indiana University Press, 2008.

____________. "History Matters." In Manju Jain (ed), *Narratives of Indian Cinema*. New Delhi: Primus Books, 2009, pp. 53–66.

Wilkinson-Weber, Clare M. *Fashioning Bollywood: The Making and Meaning of Hindi Film Costume*. London: Bloomsbury Academic, 2014.

____________. "Making Faces: Competition and Change in the Production of Bollywood Film Star Looks." In Andrew Dawson and Sean Holmes (eds), *Working in the Global Film Industries: Creativity, Systems, Space, Patronage*. London: Bloomsbury Academic, 2012 (N page. Kindle edition).

____________. "A Need for Redress: Costume in Some Recent Hindi Film Remakes." In *BioScope: South Asian Screen Studies*, Vol. 1, No. 2, July 2010, pp. 125–45.

Willis, Andrew. "Locating Bollywood: Notes on the Hindi Blockbuster, 1975 to the Present." In Stringer, Julian (ed), *Movie Blockbusters*. London: Routledge, 2003, pp. 255–68.

FILMOGRAPHY

BHUVAN SHOME (Mrinal Sen, India, 1969), Voiceover (as Amitabh)
SAAT HINDUSTANI (Khwaja Ahmad Abbas, India, 1970), Anwar Ali Anwar
ANAND (Hrishikesh Mukherjee, India, 1971), Dr. Bhaskar K. Bannerjee/Babu Moshai
PARWANA (Jyoti Swarup, India, 1971), Kumar Sen
PYAR KI KAHANI (Ravee Nagaich, India, 1971), Ram G. Chandra
RESHMA AND SHERA (Sunil Dutt, India, 1971), Chhotu
BANSI BIRJU (Prakash Verma, India, 1972), Birju
BAWARCHI (Hrishikesh Mukherjee, India, 1972), Voiceover
BOMBAY TO GOA (S. Ramanathan, India, 1972), Ravi Kumar
EK NAZAR (B.R. Ishara, India, 1972), Manmohan Akash Tyagi
GARAM MASALA (Aspi Irani, India, 1972), Robert Taylor (Uncredited)
JABAN (Palash Bannerjee, India, 1972), Dalaljit
PIYA KA GHAR (Basu Chatterjee, India, 1972), Guest Appearance
RAASTE KAA PATTHAR (Mukul Dutt, India, 1972), Jai Shankar Rai
SANJOG (S.S. Balan, India 1972), Mohan
ABHIMAAN (Hrishikesh Mukherjee, India, 1973), Subir Kumar (Beeru)
BANDHE HAATH (O.P. Goyle, India, 1973), Shyamu & Deepak
GEHRI CHAAL (C.V. Sridhar, India, 1973), Ratan
NAMAK HARAAM (Hrishikesh Mukherjee, India, 1973), Vikram (Vicky) Maharaj

SAUDAGAR (Sudhendu Roy, India, 1973), Moti
ZANJEER (Prakash Mehra, India, 1973), Insp. Vijay Khanna
BENAAM (Narinder Bedi, India, 1974), Amit Srivastav
DOST (Dulal Guha, India, 1974), Anand (uncredited)
KASAUTI (Arabind Sen, India, 1974), Amitabh (Amit) Sharma
KUNWARA BAAP (Mehmood, India, 1974), Augustine
MAJBOOR (Ravi Tandon, India, 1974), Ravi Khanna
PARINAY (Kantilal Rathod, India, 1974), Voiceover
ROTI KAPADA AUR MAKAAN (Manoj Kumar, India, 1974), Vijay
CHUPKE CHUPKE (Hrishikesh Mukherjee, India, 1975), Professor Sukumar Sinha
DEEWAAR (Yash Chopra, India, 1975), Vijay Verma
FARAAR (Shanker Mukherjee, India, 1975), Rajesh (Raj)
MILI (Hrishikesh Mukherjee, India, 1975), Shekhar Dayal
SHOLAY (Ramesh Sippy, India, 1975), Jai
ZAMEER (Ravi Chopra, India, 1975), Badal
AADALAT (Narinder Bedi, India, 1975), Thakur Dharam Chand 'Dharma' & Raju
CHHOTI SI BAAT (Basu Chatterjee, India, 1975), Himself (uncredited)
BALIKA BADHU (Tarun Majumdar, India, 1976), Adult Amal (voiceover)
DO ANJAANE (Dulal Guha, India, 1976), Amit Roy/Naresh Dutt
HERA PHERI (Prakash Mehra, India, 1976), Vijay
KABHI KABHI (Yash Chopra, India, 1976), Amitabh Malhotra
ALAAP (Hrishikesh Mukherjee, India, 1977), Alok Prasad
AMAR AKBAR ANTHONY (Manmohan Desai, India, 1977), Anthony Gonzalves
CHARANDAS (B.S. Thapa, India, 1977), Liyaqat Ali Qawwal
IMAAN DHARAM (Desh Mukerji, India, 1977), Ahmad Reza
KHOON PASINA (Rakesh Kumar, India, 1977), Shiva/Tiger
PARVARISH (Manmohan Desai, India, 1977), Amit
THE CHESS PLAYERS (Satyajit Ray, India, 1977), Voiceover
BESHARAM (Deven Verma, India, 1978), Ram Kumar Chandra/ Prince Chandrashekar

DON (Chandra Barot, India, 1978), Don & Vijay

GANGA KI SAUGAND (Sultan Ahmad, India, 1978), Jeeva

KASME VAADE (Ramesh Behl, India, 1978), Amit & Shankar

MUQADDAR KA SIKANDAR (Prakash Mehra, India, 1978), Sikandar

TRISHUL (Yash Chopra, India 1978), Vijay Kumar

AHSAAS (Surindara Suri, India, 1979), Uncredited

JURMANA (Hrishikesh Mukherjee, India, 1979), Inder Saxena

KAALA PATTHAR (Yash Chopra, India, 1979) Vijay Pal Singh

MANZIL (Basu Chatterjee, India, 1979), Ajay Chandra

MR. NATWARLAL (Rakesh Kumar, India, 1979), Natwarlal

SUHAAG (Manmohan Desai, India, 1979), Amit Kapoor

THE GREAT GAMBLER (Shakti Samanta, India, 1979), Jay & Inspector Vijay

GOL MAAL (Hrishikesh Mukherjee, India, 1979), Himself

RAM BALRAM (Vijay Anand, India, 1980), Inspector Balram Singh

DO AUR DO PAANCH (Rakesh Kumar, India, 1980), Vijay /Ram

DOSTANA (Raj Khosla, India, 1980), Vijay Varma

SHAAN (Ramesh Sippy, India, 1980), Vijay Kumar

BARSAAT KI EK RAAT (Shakti Samanta, India, 1981), Inspector Abhijeet Rai

COMMANDER (Rakesh Kumar, India, 1981), Punjabi truck driver (uncredited)

KAALIA (Tinnu Anand, India, 1981), Kallu/Kaalia

LAAWARIS (Prakash Mehra, India, 1981), Heera

NASEEB (Manmohan Desai, India, 1981), John Jaani Janardhan

SILSILA (Yash Chopra, India, 1981), Amit Malhotra

WALAYATI BABU (Dharam Kumar, India, 1981), Jagga

YAARANA (Rakesh Kumar, India, 1981), Kishan Kumar

BEMISAL (Hrishikesh Mukherjee, India, 1982) Dr. Sudhir Roy & Adhir Roy

DESH PREMEE (Manmohan Desai, India, 1982), Master Dinanath & Raju

KHUD-DAAR (Ravi Tandon, India, 1982), Govind Srivastav/Chhotu Ustad

NAMAK HALAAL (Prakash Mehra, India, 1982), Arjun Singh
SATTE PE SATTA (Raj N. Sippy, India, 1982), Ravi Anand & Babu
SHAKTI (Ramesh Sippy, India, 1982), Vijay A. Kumar
COOLIE (Manmohan Desai & Prayag Raj, India, 1983), Iqbal A. Khan
ANDHAA KANOON (T. Rama Rao, India, 1983), Jan Nissar Akhtar Khan
MAHAAN (S. Ramanathan, India, 1983), Amit / Rana Ranveer, Guru & Insp. Shankar
NASTIK (Pramod Chakravorty, India, 1983), Shankar/Sheru & Bhola
PUKAR (Ramesh Behl, India, 1983), Ramdas/Ronnie
INQUILAAB (T. Rama Rao, India, 1984), A.C.P. Amar Nath
KANOON KYA KAREGA (Mukul Anand, India, 1984), Voiceover
KHABARDAR (T. Rama Rao, India, 1984), Doctor
PAAN KHAYE SAIYAN HAMAAR (Sujit Kumar, India, 1984), Nahar Singh
SHARAABI (Prakash Mehra, India, 1984), Vicky Kapoor
GERAFTAAR (Prayag Raj, India, 1985), Insp. Karan Kumar Khanna
GHULAMI (J.P. Dutta, India, 1985), Voiceover (uncredited)
MARD (Manmohan Desai, India, 1985), Raju Singh (Mard)
AAKHREE RAASTA (K. Bhagya Raj, India, 1986), David D'Costa & Insp. Vijay Sandaliya
GANGAA JAMUNAA SARASWATHI (Manmohan Desai, India, 1988), Ganga Prasad
SHAHENSHAH (Tinnu Anand, India, 1988), Vijay Kumar Srivastava/ Shahenshah
SOORMA BHOPALI (Jagdeep, India, 1988), Police Inspector
BATWARA (J.P. Dutta, India, 1989), Voiceover
JAADUGAR (Prakash Mehra, India, 1989), Goga
MAIN AZAAD HOON (Tinnu Anand, India, 1989), Azaad
TOOFAN (Ketan Desai, India, 1989), Toofan & Shyam
AAJ KA ARJUN (K.C. Bokadia, India, 1990), Bhim Singh
AGNEEPATH (Mukul S. Anand, India, 1990), Vijay Dinanath Chavan
NAYA ANDAZ (Kamal, India, 1990, Short), Himself
AJOOBA (Shashi Kapoor and Gennadiy Vasilev, India/Soviet Union, 1991), Ajooba/Ali

AKAYLA (Ramesh Sippy, India, 1991), Inspector Vijay Verma

HUM (Mukul S. Anand, India, 1991), Tiger/Shekhar

INDRAJEET (K.V. Raju, India, 1991), Indrajeet

ZULM KI HUKUMAT (Bharat Rangachary, India, 1992), Voiceover

KHUDA GAWAH (Mukul S. Anand, India, 1992), Baadshah Khan

AKKA (Shridhar Joshi, India, 1994), Himself

INSANIYAT (Tony Juneja, India, 1994), Inspector Amar Pal Singh

TERE MERE SAPNE (Joy Augustine, India, 1996), Voiceover (as himself)

EER BIR PHATTE (Rakeysh Omprakash Mehra, India, 1997, music video), Himself

KABHI KABHI (Uncredited, India, 1997, music video), Himself

MRITYUDAATA (Mehul Kumar, India, 1997), Dr. Ram Prasad Ghayal

BADE MIYAN CHOTE MIYAN (David Dhawan, India, 1998), Inspector Arjun Singh & Bade Miyan

HERO HINDUSTANI (Aziz Sejawal, India, 1998), Voiceover

MAJOR SAAB Major (Tinnu Anand, India, 1998), Jasbir Singh Rana

HELLO BROTHER (Sohail Khan, India, 1999), Voiceover (God)

HINDUSTAN KI KASAM (Veeru Devgan, India, 1999), Kabeera

KOHRAM (Mehul Kumar, India, 1999), Col. Balbir Singh Sodi/Devraj Hathoda/Dada Bhai

LAL BAADSHAH (K.C. Bokadia, India, 1999), Lal 'Baadshah' Singh & Ranbhir Singh

SOORYAVANSHAM (Satyanarayana E.V.V. and Pranavanand), Thakur Bhanu Pratap Singh & Heera Singh

KAUN BANEGA CROREPATI (Siddharth Basu, India, 2000. Also 2005–6; 2010, 2011, 2012, 2013, 2014, TV Quiz Show), Himself

MOHABBATEIN (Aditya Chopra, India, 2000), Narayan Shankar

AKS (Rakesh Omprakash Mehra, India, 2001), Inspector Manu Verma

EK RISHTAA: BOND OF LOVE (Suneel Darshan, India, 2001), Vijay Kapoor

KABHI KHUSHI KABHIE GHAM (Karan Johar, India, 2001), Yashvardhan Raichand

LAGAAN: ONCE UPON A TIME IN INDIA (Ashutosh Gowarikar, India, 2001), Voiceover

AANKHEN (Vipul Amrutlal Shah, India, 2002), Vijay Singh Rajput

AGNIVARSHA: THE FIRE AND THE RAIN (Arjun Sajnani, India, 2002), Indra

HUM KISI SE KUM NAHIN (David Dhawan, India, 2002), Dr. Rastogi

KAANTE (Sanjay Gupta, India, 2002), Yashvardhan 'Major' Rampal

KABHI NAHI (Uncredited, India, 2002, music video), Himself

BOOM (Kaizad Gustad, India, 2003), Bade Mia

KHUSHI (Surya S.J and Sunil Kumar Agrawal, India, 2003), Voiceover

AA AE O (Uncredited, India, 2003, music video), Himself

ARMAAN (Honey Irani, India, 2003), Dr. Siddharth Sinha

BAGHBAN (Ravi Chopra, India, 2003), Raj Malhotra

FUN2SHH... DUDES IN THE 10TH CENTURY (Imtiaz Punjabi, India, 2003), Voiceover

MUMBAI SE AAYA MERA DOST (Apoorva Lakhia, India, 2003), Voiceover

AB TUMHARE HAWALE WATAN SAATHIYO (Anil Sharma, India, 2004), Major General Amarjeet Singh

AETBAAR (Vikram Bhatt, India, 2004), Dr. Ranveer Malhotra

DEEWAAR: LET'S BRING OUR HEROES HOME (Milan Luthria, India, 2004), Maj. Ranvir Kaul

DEV (Govind Nihalani, India, 2004), JCP Dev Pratap Singh

HUM KAUN HAI? (Ravi Sharma Shankar, India, 2004), Major Frank John Williams/Frank James Williams

INSAAF: THE JUSTICE (Shrey Srivastava, India, 2004), Voiceover

KHAKEE (Rajkumar Santoshi, India, 2004), DCP Anant Kumar Shrivastav

KYUN! HO GAYA NA... (Samir Karnik, India, 2004), Raj Chauhan

LAKSHYA (Farhan Akhtar, India, 2004), Col. Sunil Damle

RUDRAKSH (Mani Shankar, India, 2004), Voiceover

VEER-ZAARA (Yash Chopra, India, 2004), Chaudhary Sumer Singh

BLACK (Sanjay Leela Bhansali, India, 2005), Debraj Sahai

BUNTY AUR BABLI (Shaad Ali Saigal, India, 2005), DCP Dashrath Singh

DIL JO BHI KAHEY... (Romesh Sharma, India, 2005), Shekhar Sinha

EK AJNABEE (Apoorva Lakhia, India, 2005), Col. Suryaveer Singh

OYE BUBBLY (Vishal Shekhar, India, 2005, Pepsi Short Advertisement Film), Himself

PAHELI (Amol Palekar, India, 2005), Gadariya

PARINEETA (Pradeep Sarkar, India, 2005), Voiceover

SARKAR (Ram Gopal Varma, India, 2005), Subhash Nagre 'Sarkar'

RAMJI LONDONWALE (Sanjay Dayma, India, 2005), Himself

VIRUDDH... FAMILY COMES FIRST (Mahesh V. Manjrekar, India, 2005), Vidhyadar Ramkrishna Patwardhan

WAQT: THE RACE AGAINST TIME (Vipul Amrutlal Shah, India, 2005), Ishwarchand Thakur

BAABUL (Ravi Chopra, India, 2006), Balraj Kapoor

DARNA ZAROORI HAI – YOU GOTTA BE SCARED (Ram Gopal Varma, India, 2006), Professor

FAMILY: TIES OF BLOOD (Rajkumar Santoshi, India, 2006), Virendra 'Viren' Sahi

GANGA (Abhishek Chhadha, India, 2006), Thakur Vijay Singh

KABHI ALVIDA NAA KEHNA (Karan Johar, India, 2006), Samarjit 'Sam' Talwar

CHEENI KUM (R. Balki, India, 2007), Buddhadev Gupta

EK KRANTIVEER: VASUDEV BALWANT PHADKE (Gajendra Ahire, India, 2007), Voiceover

EKLAVYA: THE ROYAL GUARD (Vidhu Vinod Chopra, India, 2007), Eklavya

GANGOTRI (Abhishek, India, 2007), Thakur Vijay 'Thakur Kaka' Singh

JHOOM BARABAR JHOOM (Shaad Ali, India, 2007), Dancer/Singer

NISHABD (Ram Gopal Varma, India, 2007), Vijay

RAM GOPAL VARMA KI AAG (Ram Gopal Varma, India, 2007), Babban Singh

SHOOTOUT AT LOKHANDWALA (Apoorva Lakhia, India, 2007), Dhingra

SWAMI (Ganesh Acharya, India, 2007), Voiceover

THE LAST LEAR (Rituparno Ghosh, India, 2007), Harish 'Harry' Mishra

BHOOTHNATH (Vivek Sharma, India, 2008) Kailash 'Bhoothnath' Nath

GOD TUSSI GREAT HO (Rumy Jaffry, India, 2008), God

JODHAA AKBAR (Ashutosh Gowarikar, India, 2008), Voiceover

SARKAR RAJ (Ram Gopal Varma, India, 2008), Subhash 'Sarkar' Nagare

YAAR MERI ZINDAGI (Ashok Gupta, India, 2008), Dr. Ajay Singh

ALADIN (Sujoy Ghosh, India, 2009), Genius

DELHI-6 (Rakesh Omprakash Mehra, India, 2009), Annapurna's husband

PAA (R. Balki, India, 2009), Auro

ZOR LAGAA KE... HAIYA! (Girish Girija Joshi, India, 2009), Voiceover

KANDAHAR (Major Ravi, India, 2010), Lokanatha Sharma

RANN (Ram Gopal Varma, India, 2010), Vijay Harshvardhan Malik

TEEN PATTI (Leena Yadav, India, 2010) Professor Venkat Subramaniam

AARAKSHAN (Prakash Jha, India, 2011), Prabhakar Anand

BBUDDAH... HOGA TERRA BAAP (Puri Jagannadh, India, 2011), Vijju 'Bbuddah'

BOL BACHCHAN (Rohit Shetty, India, 2012), Himself

DEPARTMENT (Ram Gopal Varma, India, 2012), Sarjerao Gaikwad

ENGLISH VINGLISH (Gauri Shinde, India, 2012), Stranger in the plane

GANGA DEVI (Abhishek Chhadha, India, 2012), Himself

BOSS (Anthony D'Souza, India, 2013), Voiceover

SATYAGRAHA (Prakash Jha, India, 2013), Dwarka Anand

KRRISH 3 (Rakesh Roshan, India, 2013), Voiceover

MAHABHARAT (Amaan Khan, India, 2013, animated), Bheeshma (voice)

THE GREAT GATSBY (Baz Luhrmann, USA, 2013), Meyer Wolfsheim

BOMBAY TALKIES/MURABBA (Anurag Kashyap, India, 2013), Himself

MANAM (Vikram K. Kumar, India, 2014), Pratap

BHOOTHNATH RETURNS (Nitesh Tiwari, India, 2014), Bhoothnath

NA UPAAYA SE KAHIN BEHTAR HAI SAAVDHAANI (Piya Sorcar, India, 2014, animated short), Doctor

PREVENTION IS BETTER THAN NO CURE (Piya Sorcar, India, 2014, animated short), Doctor

YUDH (Ribhu Dasgupta, India, 2014, TV Mini-Series), Yudhishthir Sikarwar

GIRL RISING INDIA: WOH PADHEGI, WOH UDEGI (Indrani Pal-Chaudhuri, India, 2015), Himself

PIKU (Shoojit Sircar, India, 2015), Bhaskor Banerjee

SHAMITABH (R. Balki, India, 2015), Amitabh Sinha/Shamitabh

KI AND KA (R. Balki, India, 2016), Himself

TE3N (Ribhu Dasgupta, India, 2016), John Biswas

WAZIR (Bejoy Nambiar, India, 2016), Pandit Omkarnath Dhar

Additional Filmography

RAJA HARISHCHANDRA (D.G. Phalke, India, 1913)

DEVDAS (P.C. Barua, India, 1935)

A PLACE IN THE SUN (George Stevens, USA, 1951)

LIMELIGHT (Charles Chaplin, USA, 1952)

THE WILD ONE (Laslo Benedek, USA, 1953)

JAGRITI (Satyen Bose, India, 1956)

THE APARTMENT (Billy Wilder, USA, 1960)

AN ANGRY YOUNG MAN (Shamsuddin, India, 1970, short)

KHOOBSURAT (Hrishikesh Mukherjee, India, 1980)

KARZ (Subhash Ghai, India, 1980)

PREM ROG (Raj Kapoor, India, 1982)

CHAKRAVYUHA (V. Somasekhar, India, 1983)

KHOON BHARI MAANG (Rakesh Roshan, India, 1988)
QAYAMAT SE QAYAMAT TAK (Mansoor Khan, India, 1988)
MAINE PYAR KIYA (Sooraj R. Barjatya, India, 1989)
PHOOL BANE ANGAAREY (K.C. Bokadia, India, 1991)
DARR (Yash Chopra, India, 1993)
BAAZIGAR (Abbas-Mustan, India, 1993)
MISTAR KARATAH (Mohamed Khan, Egypt, 1993)
ANJAAM (Rahul Rawail, India, 1994)
HUM AAPKE HAIN KAUN...! (Sooraj R. Barjatya, India, 1994)
DILWALE DULHANIYA LE JAYENGE (Aditya Chopra, India, 1995)
GHULAM (Vikram Bhatt, India, 1998)
THE MATRIX (The Wachowski Brothers, USA, 1999)
KAHO NAA ... PYAAR HAI (Rakesh Roshan, India, 2000)
MAIN HOON NA (Farah Khan, India, 2004)
DON (Farhan Akhtar, India, 2006)
OM SHANTI OM (Farah Khan, India, 2007)
SLUMDOG MILLIONAIRE (Danny Boyle & Loveleen Tandon, UK, 2008)
AGNEEPATH (Karan Malhotra, India, 2012)
GANGS OF WASSEYPUR (Anurag Kashyap, India, 2012)

INDEX

Note: n = endnote number

T